MAGI an STEPS

The Making of an Industrial Hamlet

ALAN J BROOKE

HONLEY CIVIC SOCIETY

MAGDALE and STEPS

© Alan J Brooke and Honley Civic Society

Text © Alan J Brooke

The author has asserted his moral right in accordance with Section 77 of the Copyright, Designs and Patents Act 1988.

Design PFM

Published in England by Honley Civic Society

Printed by Enterprise Print, Honley

First published privately in 2008
This expanded and revised edition published by Honley Civic Society in 2018
www.honleycivicsociety.co.uk

ISBN-13 978-1-9997663-2-0

Further published work by Alan J Brooke

Honley Socialist Club - Popular Socialism in a Yorkshire Textile Village c1891 to 1927
Colliers and Hurriers - Working Conditions in Coalmines of the Huddersfield area c1800 to 1870
The Hall Of Science - Socialism and Co-operation c1830 to 1850
The Handloom Fancy Weavers
Liberty or Death Republicans Radicals and Luddites c1793 to 1820 (with Lesley Kipling)
https://undergroundhistories.wordpress.com/

Thomas Beaumont's 1829 painting of Magdale.

MAGDALE and STEPS

PREFACE

Indigenous to Honley soil, love for my native place has prompted me to write its history before old scenes fade into the background and the old is changed into the new.

Mary Jagger - History of Honley 1914

Like Mrs Jagger, my motivation for writing this book arises from a deep attachment to the area, the Brooke family having lived at Magdale for well over 200 years. I hope my strong sense of place and the local knowledge and insights I have accumulated will enrich this account and make it of interest to all who love Magdale - native, incomer or visitor - and who want to know more about the people and forces which shaped it.

Magdale is an example of a community which represents, in microcosm, the great transformation wrought by the industrial revolution. Although it rarely exceeded 200 people at any one time, the diversity of the population, from mill owners to agricultural labourers, reflects a broad spectrum of social and economic conditions. Only a few of those left any record, but pieced together they illustrate many aspects of society and culture from the late 18th to the early 20th centuries. For this reason it is hoped that this book is not just a parochial study but also of use to those who are interested in the period in general and the Yorkshire textile industry in particular.

As well as poor handloom weavers or factory workers, who have left little more than their name, we will meet people who contributed to natural history, technological innovation, music and art. Inevitably, details about some of the more mundane yet vital aspects of people's lives are missing - but this reflects a paradox facing all histories. The commonplace is more likely to be taken for granted and consequently not recorded, while the extraordinary makes the news. I have tried to keep as near to a continuous narrative as the often scattered and fragmentary evidence will allow, in order both to describe the changes that took place and to make it as readable as possible. My own view of history is that it is important to understand the broad sweep of events, but the delight is often in the detail. We can sometimes gain as great an insight into the human condition through a single event in the life of one individual as we can through pages of historical analysis and arid statistics.

ACKNOWLEDGEMENTS

I believe that historical research is really a co-operative effort and I must acknowledge the help I have received. My comrade and friend Lesley Kipling used her many years at the local history library to pass on any information she came across. Her discovery of the obituary of my great-uncle Hamlet Brooke in particular was a stimulus to completing this research and also set me off on another rewarding project on working-men naturalists. David and John Boocock, grandsons of my great-uncle Norman Brooke, have done extensive, detailed research into the Brooke genealogy and related families and have shared that with me. They have also kindly provided me with family photos, and permission to use what I required for this book. David Bothwell of Magdale put me on the track of the Elgar connection, which has added another fascinating facet to the Magdale story. Neil Littlewood, also of Magdale, provided the important historical photo of Harry Ferguson and the post card of Nan Hob spring. Local historian Jennifer Stead uncovered the Haigh letters and passed on a transcript which reveals vivid details of life on Magdale. Roger Bird of Oakland California and his cousin Lloyd Gledhill similarly provided me with a copy of Joseph Gledhill's letter. Neville Sheard, whose father was born on Magdale, helped with the interpretation of a conveyance which throws some light on the disposal of the Dartmouth estate property. A former Magdale resident, Lesley Abernethy, has kindly shared her own research on the area for inclusion in the new edition. Bob Hirst provided photos of the Beaumont portraits still displayed in Wilshaw Church schoolroom, adding an extra human dimension to their tragic story. Above all I must thank my late father Jeffrey Brooke for a wealth of anecdotes and reminiscences, which sometimes draw on local tradition going back over a century.

There is also the debt to the many people who have devoted themselves to conserving Magdale as an amenity for the community, including the Honley Village Trust and the former Piscatorial Society, as well as numerous individuals who have done their bit to retain the character of the place. Without the preservation of the stones and structures of Magdale this history would have much less resonance. It is also a reminder that we are not celebrating a piece of 'heritage', but a living community.

Finally, I must thank Peter Marshall and Honley Civic Society. Without their encouragement and support this new edition would never have appeared.

Alan Brooke
Magdale
September 2018

Business card of Norman Brooke.

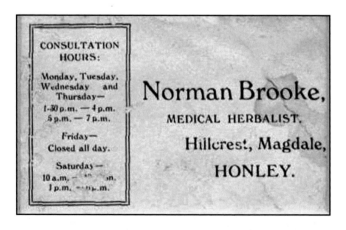

ORIGINS

Apart from a few mounds, earthworks and tracks in the woods around Magdale which could be of iron-age origin, two hidden hoards of coins are our earliest firm evidence for human activity in the locality. One, found in 1893 in Stones Wood near the cemetery, contained both British and Roman coins, possibly hidden at the time of Roman invasion of the area in the early 70s AD. Not far away, at Thirstin in the 18th century, Roman coins of a later period were uncovered. The choice of Magdale and vicinity as a hiding place would seem to indicate that in Romano-British times it was regarded as a secluded area, yet was not too far from human settlement. This still seems to have been the case during the civil war in the late 1640s, when another coin hoard was secreted in Spring Wood, where it remained until 1892. Even after the Angles made the 'clearing in the wood', which gave Honley its name, it is unlikely that the steep rocky slopes of Magdale offered any enticement to early settlers or agriculturalists. During the later Middle Ages the clearing of water meadows in the valley bottoms and of pasture on the gentler slopes was probably the first human intrusion.[1]

The name Magdale does not occur until the late 1830s, but the element 'Mag' in local place names is found as early as the mid 1400s. Local place name expert, Dr George Redmonds, found the first known reference in an agreement of 1455 between John Beaumont and Sir Richard Beaumont allowing a dam on 'magwatre' to power a fulling mill. It is appropriate that this first mention should be associated with a mill, since, as we shall see, mills played a central role in the shaping of Magdale. The 'magwatre', or Mag Dyke, or Mag Brook, as it was known by the 18th century, provided a natural boundary between the manors and later townships of Honley and South Crosland. Its alternative name, since it flowed past Crosland Hall, was sometimes simply Hall Dyke.

Magdale was part of a subdivision of the manor of Honley known as Mag Lordship, an administrative description it retained until the 1891 census. Dr Redmonds suggested that both the origin of the name Mag and of the lordship comes from Margaret Beaumont of Crosland Hall who, in the period 1356-71, was involved in an inheritance dispute following her husband John's death. This may have led to a division of the manor and the creation of the lordship consequently known, along with the river marking its boundary, by the diminutive of Margaret - Mag.[2]

There is another theory which derives Mag from the Old Norse word for 'gut', or narrow winding valley, but this is not a common place name element. However, a topographical explanation for another name for our locality, subsumed only in recent times under the name Magdale, is more likely. Steps is apparently from 'staups' indicating a hollow, which describes perfectly the situation where the valley of the River Holme swings from its northerly course almost due west, a few hundred yards north of its confluence with the Mag. Steep hills rise to the north and east, while to the west the spur between the two rivers creates the impression of a basin. However it could be that the 'steps' referred to were a river crossing, although it is hard to see where this could be given the depth of the bed of the Holme River from the banks in the vicinity of the mill. There could have been an early step crossing of the Honley road over the Mag above the weir where the footbridge was later built.[3]

The locality described here does here not cover the whole of the Mag Lordship, but only the small part now popularly known as Magdale. This extends only a few hundred yards, from Steps to Magbridge, bounded on the east by the railway embankment and on the west by Spring Wood. On the south it is delineated by the Mag river and on the

Steps Bridge before the 1980s widening, showing the date stone (*inset*) in situ above the arch.

north by the ridge of appropriately named sandstone Rough Rock, which runs eastwards from Netherton Moor, sloping steeply down towards the Mag on its south side and to a dried up stream bed in Nan Hobb Wood and the valley bottom of the River Holme on the north. The 1933 geological survey describes it as 'a pretty wooded gorge known as Mag-a-dale'![4]

The first recorded residents appear in the Almondbury parish registers of Elizabethan times. On 12th January, 1586 a Joannes Berie, ie John Berry, of Magwodde, was buried at the age of 72. An Edward Berye appears in 1593, in the record of the death of his wife Agnes and is probably the same Edward Bury 'of the Maggwood' mentioned the following year in the Honley Rental of John Kay's Woodsome estate. A Richard Taylor 'of the Wood…' may also refer to Magwood. The number and location of the 16th century dwellings is not recorded and there is no archaeological evidence which provides a clue. Presumably they were between Magbridge and Steps, in the area still referred to in the 19th century as Magwood. They were probably timber frame buildings and would leave little record, especially if the same sites were subsequently built on.[5]

More names occur in the following century, although specific references to the locality are still few. In 1620 (17th August) Johannis Hirst de Magwod was buried and in 1637 a daughter of Godfrey Heyworth was baptised. Anna the wife of a John Milnes of Magwood was buried in 1687, by which time the spelling of the place name has become standardised. There is an intriguing series of entries relating to John Sykes of Magwood. In 1689 a son, John was baptised. When his daughter Alice was baptised in 1691 his abode is given as Magbridge, perhaps showing that the place names were interchangeable. Domestic tragedy is revealed by subsequent entries. In 1696 a miscarried child was buried, followed two years later by an illegitimate (spurius) son Benjamin, born to John Sykes and Mary Lintwait, 'alias Sykes'. In 1688 the name Beaumont occurs with the baptism of Anna, the daughter of Henry and a decade later an Abraham Beaumont married Mary France, who suffered a series of three stillbirths over the next three years. Instead of Magwood, the 1701 record places the family at Magbridge. This place name also occurs in 1691 on the occasion of the burial of Thomas Lee - pauper.

STEPS MILL AND THE ROBERTS

According to Mary Jagger, a fulling mill is mentioned at Steps as early as the mid 14th century and there seems to have been one on the estate of John Kaye in the 16th century, but we do not have any definite identification until 1642 when Step Milne is recorded in the parish register with the burial of Abraham Robert's wife. Just over two months later, there is an entry for the marriage of an Abraham Roberts to Jane Taylor, although this could have been a different Abraham, since it was a family name. The Roberts family were to be associated with Steps Mill until the 1790s. In 1707 James Roberts of Steps Milne and Joseph Roberts of Dungeon Milne leased a fulling milne at Meltham from Joseph Radclife for 21 years at the annual rent of £11 a year. They were also signatories to an agreement between owners and farmers of fulling mills on prices etc. that same year. The mill must have been a profitable concern since in 1759 Joseph Roberts built the elegantly arched Steps Bridge. How the river was crossed before this is not recorded. The date stone, which was formerly in the centre of the southern parapet overlooking the river, was rescued from a pile of rubble during the bridge widening in the early 1980s and built into the adjacent roadside wall.[6]

The fulling mill at this time was the hub of the woollen industry serving many small clothiers manufacturing their own cloth. Like many other ancient fulling mills, Steps Mill was to evolve into a large scale enterprise employing hundreds of workers in all stages of woollen manufacture. The story of how this transition affected the community is central to the story of Magdale.

As 'principle inhabitants' the Roberts served as Overseers of the Poor for the township of South Crosland, Abraham appearing in that role 1749 and Joseph in 1753. Abraham also loaned money to the township and the payment of interest to him is recorded in 1774. Pauper apprentices were also taken by them as required, but in 1772 Joseph signed an indenture transferring Jonathon Crosland, who had been bound to him until he was 24, to a Netherton clothier, George Armytage. Abraham is recorded as taking on one Hannah Elie. The Roberts also caused problems for the overseers. In 1770 it was recorded in the overseers accounts 'Paid to Mary Noble for a 'bastard child' which she had by Abraham Roberts the younger at 9d a week...' Four years later it was recorded that 8d a week was being paid to Sarah Harrison for a child by Abraham Roberts senior! There is also a reference to a bastard of John, son of Joseph Roberts.[7]

OVERSEERS OF THE POOR

Although some entries in the overseers accounts are a bit cryptic they throw some interesting light on our area. Magbridge figures prominently, since paupers supported by the township rates were housed there. In 1767 payment is recorded for taking elderly Ann Dyson's goods to Magg Bridge, followed by a series of entries spanning seven years relating to her movements, buying her clothes and furnishings, or repairing the property. In December 1790, the payment of three and a half year's rent for Magbridge house of £2.19s.6d is recorded. The annual rent of 17s was evidently due before Christmas each year, but why these arrears had accumulated is not explained. For 21st December, 1793 the overseer recorded 'My gate (i.e. journey) and expenses when I paid Lord Dartmouth rent for Magbridge Houses'. This is a reminder that the estate of Kaye of Woodsome, embracing much of the Maglordship, had passed to Dartmouth in the 1720s.

In 1791, the case of 'John Brook's lame lad' is first mentioned and over the following four years efforts to place him as an apprentice are recorded. Whether he was the son of a John Brook who lived at Magbridge is not clear. The reference in the accounts for

Magbridge Cottages, c. 1980.

Healdy Butts, c 1970.

October 1793 - "paid to constable for going with me to Magbridge to bring Brook lame lad to his master", may indicate that the boy was staying in the pauper's house. A pair of crutches was bought for him for 4d. while the following March his master, Joseph Saxton, was paid the town's allowance for taking him on as an apprentice, his name now recorded as Paul Brook.[8]

As well as looking after the maintenance of illegitimate children and the poor, the overseer's duties included serving warrants – Joseph Shaw of Magwood received one in 1767 for an undisclosed reason – and certifying people to stay in the township. In 1794 he had a wasted journey for which he claimed expenses for 'My gate and chapelwarden with me to Magwood to get the soldier John Haigh sworn to his settlement but he was not at home.'

HEALDY BUTTS

That people from a different township were seeking settlement would seem to point to a growing population, or at least one that was more geographically mobile as the economy expanded. We know new dwellings were being erected in Magwood from a later reference in the Dartmouth estate terrier to Yealdy Butts cottages built in 1761.

Yealdy Butts, or Healdy Butts, comes from the old English word helde meaning a sloping place which is an accurate description of the area just downstream of Magbridge where the valley widens out to a loop in the river. Butts can either denote tree stumps, from the time it was being cleared, or a place where archery was practised. The name later appears as Healy Butts and by the late 19th century has become corrupted to its' current name 'Early Butts', reinforcing the popular belief that this was where bowmen trained in the 'olden' days. The cottages which were two-roomed are different from later buildings, being particularly low roofed, with massive door lintels and recessed mullions in the windows. The first persons associated specifically with this place are the Oldfield family. Benjamin, son of Matthew Oldfield of Healdy Butts, was buried on 25th February, 1783 and another son, Joseph, the following day. Matthew's elder brother James Oldfield, also of Healdy Butts, was buried on 24th May, 1787 aged 40. Eighteen days earlier when his last son, Matthew, was baptised, the residence was given as Maggwood, indicating that the name was possibly still interchangeable with Healdy Butts. If so, then David Taylor, a clothier who is recorded as residing at Healdy Butts in 1788 when his son George was baptised, may in fact also have been living here eight years before, at the time of the baptism of his son Joseph when their dwelling place is simply called Magwood.

The land and cottages were owned by Joseph Roberts, whose name appears on the Land Tax return for 1781, but by 1789 he must have died since it is entered as belonging to 'Widow Roberts'. The following year the Overseer's accounts record 'Paid Widow Oldfield of Healdy Buts a whole year rent to Mrs Roberts £1.13s'. This was the wife of the James Oldfield mentioned above. When Mrs Roberts leased the Steps Mill estate in 1795 this land was either leased along with it or bought, since the Overseers book for 1797 records: 'An account of what sums of money William Beaumont and his brother Richard Beaumont and Company has paid to the poor being overseers of the poor for Healdy Buts Farm for the year 1797'.

For 1802 the Land Tax returns show a 'Mr Hearnshaw for Healdy Butts or William Beaumont & Co.' although notices in the Leeds Mercury of 1801 announced that William Beaumont, clothier, of Healdy Butts and his co-partners, were declared bankrupt. Some land was transferred to Lord Dartmouth in 1802 from the property of William Beaumont of Healdy Butts, co-partner of Richard Beaumont and Stephen

Vickerman, with the agreement of their assignees, J. Whitaker of Lane, dyer; Jos. Tolson, Wakefield, woolstapler; John Dickinson, Huddersfield, woolstapler; and Jonathon Senior, Farnley Tyas.[10]

John Carter, a carpenter, who appears in the parish registers at Magbridge in 1775 and 1782 when sons John and David were baptised, is named as the occupier of land at Bullring and Far Croft. In 1790 he acquired a house, formerly a dyehouse at Thirstin Bottoms and converted it into a scribbling mill – one of the first in Honley. The mill was still running in 1833, powered by a small wheel of only three horsepower. If the arch in the ground floor of a house at the bottom of Thirstin (now revealed by the removal of a garden) belongs to the water wheel race, it would make this the oldest surviving mill building in the area.[11]

The name 'Bullring' is still applied today to a plot of land at Magbridge. Whether this was actually used for bull-baiting, or merely for tethering a bull there at some time, is debatable. Both the Yealdy Butts cottages and Healey Butts Meadow and allotments are recorded in the Dartmouth rental, along with Croft, Lower Hay, Upper Hay and Middle Croft fields. Charles Brook, M. Oldfield, Widow Brook and James Shaw are recorded as each renting the cottages for £2 per annum.[12]

By the end of the 18th century, the hamlet had assumed the layout it basically retains to this day. The first map with any detail, William Crossley's 1788 map of the Manor of Honley, drawn up to illustrate the allocation of land under the enclosure of the commons, shows structures at Magbridge along with those at Healdy Butts, Magwood (the top of Healdy Butts Lane) and several at Steps. The depiction of Steps is confusing, since the large L-shaped ground plan it shows is the wrong orientation for the building later famous as the location of Honley's first schoolroom. Also a structure depicted on the goit (mill race) of Steps Mill is not known from other sources. Some artistic licence might have gone into drawing the map or it shows buildings now lost.

Some of the late 18th century houses can identified from datestones. The earliest of these appears to be one of 1782 on the house at 'Owlshall', Steps Hill, now (Nos 51 and 49). One cottage at Magwood bears a tablet with, 'Built by John Hirst 1792'. A John Hirst, clothier of Magwood, is named in the parish register for 1801, when his daughter Lydia was buried. Cottages at Throstlenest carry an inscription with initials and the date 1793. Absent from the 1788 map is the three storey building halfway up the road from the top of Healdy Butts lane to the junction of Whitegate. This became known as Pogson Lane and in fact a William Pogson was recorded at Magwood in 1782 when his son Joshua was baptised. He may have lived in the first house built here in the 1790s or early 1800s. Whitegate road was laid out according to specifications in the Act to enclose Netherton Moor and the name may be a corruption of 'widegate'.[13]

There are over two dozen surnames recorded for Magbridge - Magwood - Steps from 1775 to 1803 and the 1805 Dartmouth Terrier reveals about 19 dwellings. As we would expect, the most frequent occupation is clothier along with a few fulling millers, including Thomas Beaumont of Steps who is entered in the parish register in 1780 and Joseph Hutchinson of Steps Mill, recorded both in the 1798 register and in the 1805 Terrier. Other textile occupations include cloth dresser. Abraham Roberts of Magbridge appears in 1775 and in 1780 at the baptism of his son, Walker, who was living at Pogson's Lane 70 years later. When his son Abraham was baptised in 1783 Abraham senior's occupation was classed as crape maker. The presence of Amos Hirst, a collier, who lived at Magwood from at least 1771 until his death in 1795, reminds us that early Magdale was at the centre of a coal mining area composed of many small pits in Meltham and Honley townships.

INDUSTRIALISATION

STEPS MILL – LOWER AND UPPER

One of Magdale's most characteristic and notable features is the mill dam. This is not shown on the 1788 map, confirming it was not constructed to serve the long established fulling mill at Steps but was part of a new upper mill built around 1799. Unravelling what was going on at the two mills at this time is difficult.

The fulling mill at Steps was very unusual in that two rivers, the Holme and the Mag, provided the sources of its water power. A weir on the Holme directed water through a sluice, or shuttle as it is known locally, along the mill race or goit into the Mag. Just below where this goit flowed into it, the river was dammed by another weir allowing water to be led off via a second goit to the reservoir at Steps Mill. This feat of hydraulic engineering required the construction of two masonry weirs, the one on the Mag about 15 feet high, the excavation of about 300 yards of channel which was then revetted with dressed stone and the building of three culverts, including one under the Steps Bridge road.

This provided a regular supply and a substantial fall of water to power the wheel. When this arrangement was introduced is not recorded. The weirs and watercourses and mill dam have been repaired and rebuilt over the life of the mill so there are no signs of the original construction. In 1866 the damstones on the river Holme were swept away in a flood and again 15 months later. The weir on the Mag was also damaged in the latter storm.[14]

Water powered technology in the woollen industry did not change significantly until the 1790s. In the Land Tax returns of 1792 there is an entry for Mrs Roberts for a fulling mill and farm and also for Elizabeth Roberts or Edward and Benjamin Haigh 'for a new erected wheel for Engeons', - the engines being scribbling machines. The reference to the wheel would seem to show that a new structure had also been built to house scribblers, but whether it was in, adjacent to, or some distance from, the old fulling mill is not apparent. In 1795 when Mrs Roberts advertised the fulling mill at Steps 'To Let' it was described as 'in excellent repair' suggesting work had recently been done on it. The two streams of water were a selling point, powering three water wheels, six fulling stocks and three drivers, with room to set up more. The mill 'is capable of doing a great quantity of work'. The house, barn and other outbuildings of Steps Farm were also advertised 'Likewise nine days work of Land more or less near the mill in good condition…' The advert concluded, 'The situation is very eligible and in a very populous manufacturing part of the country, lies near to the turnpike road and is only three miles from Huddersfield'.[15]

There is no mention of scribbling engines, but in 1797 the Land Tax returns refer to William Beaumont & Co for Steps Mill and farm (£1.7s.11d, as well as, as we have seen for Healdy Butts, 13s 10d) and also Edward Haigh for Engeons,18s. William Beaumont of Steps is recorded as receiving the allowance of 10s 6d for taking a town's apprentice in 1796, so he presumably took over the lease from that date. In 1800 Beaumont was balloted to serve in the militia, but he was wealthy enough to pay for another man to take his place. In June the township overseer recorded paying £15 to the Huddersfield overseer as an allowance for William Crosland's wife 'Her husband being a substitute for William Beaumont of Steps.'

Magdale mill dam looking west.

Upper Steps Millwheel, revealed during demolition prior to the First World War.

By 1800 we know that two mills were in existence from a Royal Exchange Insurance policy covering Steps Mill for £600 and Upper Steps Mill for £200. Despite, as we have seen, being declared bankrupt in 1801, Beaumont had by 1805 again leased Steps Mill from the Dartmouth estate. The Terrier list describes 'A Scribbling & Slubbing mill of 3 floors & weaving shops built by tenant 6 Years ago.' and also ' A large stone and slate scribbling and slubbing mill of three floors driven by three wheels.'

The three wheels accord with the description in the 1795 advert, but this would indicate that a new structure was built around 1799. The mention of weaving shops is particularly tantalising, since weaving on the mill premises was still an uncommon innovation. The confusion is compounded by a summary in the Terrier of property leased to Beaumont comprising 'A large fulling and scribbling mill with a detached cotton mill. Likewise several Dwelling Houses & cottages, barns and outbuildings. Altogether forming the appearance of a Manufactory on a large scale'.[16]

The cotton factory must have been located at Upper Steps Mill, hence its description as detached. In 1803, the *Leeds Mercury* (9th April) announced the dissolution of the partnership, lately carried on at Steps Mill in Honley by William Bailey the Elder of Batty Mill, Kirkheaton, Richard Brown, Huddersfield and William Bailey the younger of Honley, Cotton Spinners.

A few months later, on 1st October, Richard Brown, shear-grinder of Close House and William Bailey, maltster, of Battye Ford, described as traders of cotton warps, assigned the mill and machinery in security for loans of £2,500 to Ben Ingham of Lockwood, Joshua Ingham of Mirfield and Silvester Sikes, Huddersfield, bankers. Interestingly the name is given as Healdy Butts Mill, South Crosland.[17]

The inventory lists the machinery in a building of five floors along with a warehouse or outbuilding, including a stretching frame, a drawing frame, two carding machines, ten spinning frames, nine twisting frames, three warping frames and one reeling frame. Bailey and Brown are still recorded in the 1804 Land Tax returns for the cotton factory but this does not tell us whether it was in production or not.

Referring to a mill at Slaithwaite which converted from woollen to cotton around 1802 (Ingham & Sikes were again involved) the Dartmouth Terrier explained that it was the result of 'the spirit of erecting cotton mills being high at that time'. The speculative nature of the enterprise is underlined by the fact both Brown & Bailey had other non-cotton related businesses. In 1805 the final dissolution of the partnership of William Bailey & Co., cotton spinners of Steps Mill, was announced, advertising the sale of machinery by private contract as it stood on the premises;

> *this machinery is entirely new and fully complete for twisting the warps, reeling and every other part of the spinning business on a moderately extensive scale...N.B. the above is a desirable situation in the midst of the Woollen Manufactory.*

added the advert, as if acknowledging that prospects for it continuing as a cotton factory were limited.[18]

Since it is clear that the Steps cotton factory and the Healdy Butts Mill are one and the same it seems safe to assume that this refers to Upper Steps Mill which began life spinning cotton around 1799. A goit was cut from the bend of the river through the meadow at Healdy Butts, passing within a few yards of the row of cottages. Just past there it widens out into the mill dam which stretches for about 150 yards. The water was directed by a sluice onto the wheel and discharged almost immediately into the goit of Lower Steps Mill. The mill dam was formed by raising an embankment which at one point rises almost directly from the river bank. Extensive stone revetment of the river

The dam from Magdale with Timinets in the centre background.

was needed to stop erosion under the dam embankment. The surface of the river falls to around ten feet below the surface of the dam which was also excavated so that, at least before it silted up, it contained a massive volume of water.

It was also cut within a few yards of the three storey, L-shaped building, with its unusual central barn-like arch and large quoining, later associated with the Upper Mill which it evidently predates. The long row of mullioned windows indicates that its top storey was intended as a weaving shop and there was also ample warehouse space. When the dam was built the road, originally level with the ground floor, was raised, or even a new one created, with wells for some of the windows on the north side of the building, now below road level. An article on Methodism in Honley in 1893, as well as Mrs Jagger's History, recalled Steps Mill's association with the Sunday school, run jointly by the Church of England, Methodists and Independents from 1790-1815, drawing teachers from as far afield as Castle Hill Side, Berry Brow, Woodroyd, Smithy Place and South Crosland. Instead of paper or slates the pupils scratched their letters in a box of Calais sand.[19]

It seems already to be subdivided into dwellings by the early 19th century and is later described as Steps Fold. With the erection of the Upper Mill, buildings were constructed against it and the shadow of the roof-line of one of these is still visible on the gable end. The 1805 Dartmouth Terrier also contains a sketch interpolated in 1829 showing the complex of buildings at the Upper Mill, including a 14-horse-power wheel, one structure of four floors plus loft and another of two floors, built on the side of the lower mill goit. An old photo, possibly as early as the 1860s, shows the extent of this building.

A further twist to the problem of untangling the different mills at Steps is added by a laconic entry in *Mayall Annals of Yorkshire* for November 1806 - 'Steps Mill near Honley was destroyed by fire'. According to the *Leeds Intelligencer* not only was the building and machinery 'entirely consumed' but also the overlooker, who lived in an adjoining house, was killed trying to fight the fire.[20]

THE POOR

The early 1800s were not just a bad time for bankrupt cotton speculators and woollen manufacturers. From 1799 to 1802 there was a period of high prices, food shortages and epidemics. Resumption of war with Napoleon in 1803 led to a serious dislocation of trade contributing to unrest which reached its peak in 1812 with the Luddite risings. The end of the war saw bad harvests, unemployment and political discontent lasting until the early 1820s. Although we do not know how directly all these events impacted on the people of Magwood and Steps it is a context we must bear in mind when examining the condition of the inhabitants.

By December 1800 the food situation was so dire that West Riding magistrates recommended that overseers of the poor distribute herrings and a shipment was ordered from Hull. In January 1801 the South Crosland overseer recorded 'Expenses for David Harrison and myself at Huddersfield meeting respecting Rice and Herrins [sic]'. The sum of 5s was claimed, suggesting that austerity measures were not applicable to some of those responsible for administering them!

The food shortage was compounded by a fever epidemic which, by the end of 1801, was virulent in the villages around Honley. Although we cannot be sure that fatalities were due to disease, hunger or their combined effects, the Almondbury parish burials register show an exceptionally high death rate in some localities at this time. Charles Wood, clothier of Magwood, buried his wife Mary on 30th April, 1800 and his daughter Mary on 28th June. Charles Lodge, a tailor of Magwood buried his infant son on 15th May, 1800 followed the next year by his wife Ellen and daughter Sarah on the 3th and 10th May. These could have been usual childbirth and infant deaths, but, totalled with the others for these years, it seems to be a high number for such a small hamlet. They include:

1800
16 May: *Charles son of John Donkersley, Magwood, clothier (christened the previous September)*
16 May: *Joseph, son of James Collier, of Magwood, clothier;*
17 May: *an unbaptised child of John Donkersley,*
5 December: *Hannah, daughter of John Kinder of Magwood, cloth dresser.*

1801
28 June: *Lydia daughter of John Hirst, of Magwood,,clothier*
19 July: *Hannah daughter of Ben Oldfield of Magwood, clothier*
26 August: *unbaptised child of Joseph Grime of Magwood, clothier.*
15 December: *Sally daughter of David Carter of Magbridge, carpenter. (baptised a little more than two weeks previously).*

Neighbouring areas, such as Reins, also appear to record a higher mortality in this period.

By now the rent for the pauper house at Magbridge had risen to one guinea a year. The entries in the overseers' accounts continue to be brief and it is not apparent whether recipients of relief were living there, or in their own homes. In March and April 1801 weekly payments, varying from 2s.6d to 4s a week, are entered for the wife of John Oldfield of Magwood. Whether this is because he was sick, or serving away as a soldier, is not revealed. A John Oldfield was also receiving payments in 1812 - in January his abode is described as Magbridge, in February as Magwood, so again it is not clear where he lived. In 1807 a Mary Brook of Magbridge was receiving relief, including the purchase of a pair of shoes for her, and two years later David Parkin was paid 'for cart and horse fetching Mary Brook from Magbridge to Crosland.' She was the possibly the same as the Widow Brook receiving relief at Magbridge in February 1812, since Mary is recorded there again the following month. Widow Brook was still receiving relief, as well as 3s.9d for 'cloth for a shift', in 1815.

Evidence that residents were involved in the political turmoil of the times, particularly the abortive uprising of 1817, comes from the lists of those committed to York Castle for 'tumultuously assembling'. After attempting to seize arms in Honley they marched on Huddersfield and clashed with the Yeomanry. Abraham Oldfield, a weaver of Steps and John Oldfield, weaver of Magbridge are both named. These are probably cousins, but the age of both is wrongly given as 31. The overseer records 12s paid to Abraham Oldfield's wife in 1817 to support her, although it does not refer to his imprisonment. All the insurgents were acquitted due to public sympathy and a belief they had been victims of a government agent provocateur. One who reputedly narrowly missed arrest was the most famous pupil of Steps Sunday school, the cloth dresser Abraham Lockwood, later the local Methodist preacher renowned as the Bishop of Berry Brow.[21]

There are few relevant entries in the Overseers' book for almost a decade until in March 1826, a 'Journey to Magbridge to see about proping Mary Brook house' and a payment to John Carter 'for the house proping' is recorded. Presumably this means propping of a house in serious disrepair and subsequent references point clearly to this being the pauper's house. Expenses were paid on 1st May for someone 'going to Huddersfield to meet Ld Dartmouth Steward about Magbrigg House' and over the following months several disbursements were made for its renovation.

> 10 May: a man one days wages for sorting slates and stones and removing out of Magbrigg House 2s.6d
>
> 5 June: estimate of repairs of Magbrigg House 4s
>
> 15 June: two journeys to Magbrigg about the building 2s
>
> 16 June: wage and expenses for Joseph Mellor and Self removing Mary Brook and her goods to Delph 3s.6d. [another house rented by the township for paupers at Delph near Armitage Bridge].
>
> 23 June: estimate to Magbridge House plastering 1s
>
> 4 July: gate to Berry Brow to plasterer to get forward with house at Magbridge

Work done on the building repairs totalled £14.15s. plus windows, doors and glazing £5.16s. 2d and plastering £2.13s.11d.

The last reference to the house is for 6d paid to John for mending the lock in April 1827. After the enactment of the Act in 1834 establishing a new system of administering poor relief, the house was no longer required and was one of five rented out by Dartmouth to private tenants. Which one of the present cottages at Magbridge this was, if indeed it still survives, is impossible to say.

PARKTON GROVE

Parkton Grove house, set just to the east of the old turnpike, now Hangingstone road, plays an important part in the story of Steps and the development of the textile industry. It was built by the fancy cloth manufacturer John Oldfield, probably not long before his marriage in September 1819 to Ann, the daughter of Cowling Ackroyd of Bradford. While it was being built he invited John Nowell of Farnley Wood, a self taught chemist and polymath, to visit and advise him on a revolutionary new method of heating dyeing vats by steam, invented by Nowell and demonstrated at his father William's works at Birks mill, Almondbury. A dyeworks and other buildings were built near the house and as a result of his meeting with Nowell, Oldfield

was bold enough to adopt there, the plan of steam dyeing, with great success into the fancy trade of this neighbourhood, a method admirably adapted to the delicate tints and colours requisite in that trade...to him be given the honour of introducing, on this large scale, a process now become general.

The early 1820s were boom years for the fancy trade and John Oldfield is listed as one of those having a stand at Huddersfield Cloth Hall in 1823.[22]

However, prosperity was short lived and the collapse of national and local banks in 1826 led to the failure of several fancy manufacturers and widespread unemployment. Oldfield, acting as secretary, was among 30 manufacturers and others who convened a meeting on 11th December, 1829 at the Court House in Huddersfield 'to take into consideration the present deplorable state of the Operatives and Labouring Classes in consequence of the extreme Depression of Trade.' Oldfield was chosen as one of the committee to put the decisions of the meeting on relieving the poor into effect. He also became involved in a dispute with the Rev. Franks, vicar of Huddersfield, who claimed that he had been mislead about the objectives of the meeting - instead of focusing on the issue of charity it had descended into a political debate on government policies such as taxes and paper money. On 24th December, Oldfield wrote to the *Leeds Mercury* in response to a letter from the Rev. Franks, which he felt conveyed 'insinuations unfavourable to my character.' The argument with Franks must have been resolved since the following year both men served on a committee to call for the abolition of slavery in the colonies.[23]

Oldfield's family suffered a traumatic time in the summer of 1828 when his 'little boy' was bitten on the arm by a dog. Although only a slight wound, the dog which belonged to a Meltham butcher had also bitten five other people and about 20 dogs before being shot in a field at South Crosland since it was feared that it was suffering from rabies. As a precaution 'excision and cautery' was applied to the boys wound. Although no one was infected such periodic scares caused great alarm and an anxious wait to see if symptoms developed in those attacked.[24]

Sadly, John Oldfield was not to live to see his little son grow up. He died in 1832. The following year the sale notice for Parkton Grove describes it as a desirable five-bedroom residence situated on an eminence commanding beautiful views of the surrounding country, with a yard, barn, stable, coach house and mistal along with several neat cottages, a warehouse, workshops, dyehouse and wool drying stove, suitable for an extensive business, along with several acres of land. The house was eventually acquired by Joshua Beaumont of Steps Mill but the related buildings were cleared away and whatever remained of them buried under the railway embankment, leaving no trace of this once important industrial site.[25]

Parkton Grove.

Steps Mill.

1830s & 40s – AN ARTIST,
MANUFACTURERS AND CHARTISTS

Shortly after the first edition of this book was published the author was contacted by a London art collector who had acquired a painting bearing the inscription on the back of the canvas, 'Steps near Honley. Painted by Thomas Beaumont 20 July 1829'. There is also an illegible motto in Latin. Is this the Thomas Beaumont who appears in the 1830 Trade Directory as 'overlooker, Steps', and if so, was he member of the Beaumont family who leased Upper Steps Mill? The picture, although in a naïve, primitivist style and not a realist portrayal of the scene, clearly shows Upper Steps Mill with an exposed water wheel and shafting. This must be the 14hp wheel recorded on the plan interpolated in the Dartmouth Terrier in 1829. The housing for the wheel which appears in later photos must have been built after this date. The conglomeration of buildings built up against the gable of the L – shaped 'school house' is also depicted in the painting, very much as it appears on the earliest photo we have of the mill. To have a ground plan of a mill and a contemporary pictorial record at such an early period is quite unusual.

In front of that building, in the land between the houses and the mill dam, (known as Steps Green), there are eight rows of tenters and a tiny figure is visible tentering a length of cloth. A cow and some domestic fowls, either hens or geese, are shown by the dam side. The 'hebble' footbridge over the Mag can also be seen but it is not in proportion.

Although the perspective of the painting is not accurate, the road appears to run beside the ground floor of the 'schoolhouse' making the raising of the road level with the top story of the building later, and not associated with the works related to the creation of the dam. The gardens between the front of the houses and the road appear to be longer than today but, again, this may be due to faulty perspective. There was a barn-like building attached to the small house at Throstlenest (later No.35 Magdale) on the site of Nos 33 and 31. No 55 Magdale is shown as a two storey house, so the painting provides a terminus post quem for when the extra story was added with the same fenestration as adjoining No53. As well as the person at the tenters two tiny figures are visible, one a woman near the side of the dam in a bright red dress or shawl – our first glimpse of Magdalers![26]

The 1826 financial crash led to numerous bankruptcies amongst woollen manufacturers. Hundreds of looms in Honley lay idle by 1829, forcing many weavers to subsist on only a few pence a day. One of those declared bankrupt in March 1827 was William Beaumont, who had appeared in the 1822 *Baines Trade Directory* as a scribbling miller of Steps. In the 1826 land tax returns, he was assessed for house, land and mills. On 3rd August, the Huddersfield Banking Co. stepped in to advance him £1,000 on security of the property lease and machinery at Steps Mill. But he seems to have given up the lease. A note in the Dartmouth Terrier added to the sketch plan of Upper Steps Mill states: 'To be let from Mayday 1829 to Joshua Beaumont, Enoch Vickerman, Benjamin Vickerman at £400 a year for 14 years.' It seems the firm leased both mills, since White's Directory of the following year refers only to Beaumont & Vickerman, scribbling and fulling millers, Steps Mill.[27]

Employers tried to bale themselves out by wage cuts, leading to the growth of trade unionism across the whole range of textile occupations. After a successful strike at the large Leeds firm of Benjamin Gott in 1832 some local firms, including E. & B.

One of the earliest photographs of Steps Mill and Parkton Grove.

Both Steps Mills around 1904.

Vickerman, of Steps Mill, announced an increase of wages to parity with Gott's pay scale. Whether this was to forestall union activity is not clear. There was a growing militancy throughout the area not just for improved wages but also against the factory system itself, expressed by the campaign for a Ten Hours Bill to end the evils of child labour by enforcing a shorter working day.[28]

The resulting parliamentary inquiry into factory conditions led to the circulation of a questionnaire by the Factory Commissioners in 1833. Beaumont & Vickerman were among the respondents, describing in some detail their scribbling, fulling and finishing mill at Steps. They employed 57 persons - six males over 21, earning 26s, and 13 earning 21s, for a 69 hour week. Four slubbers, one willower, eight feeders, 12 piecers, and three millers were on piece-rate. Five females were employed (only one of them over 16) and there were about 20 employees aged 14 or under (ie more than a third of the workforce). In summer the mill started at 6.00am and finished at 7.30pm with a break for breakfast (8 - 8.30am), dinner (12.30 - 1.00pm) and lunch (5 - 5.30pm) although the fulling department kept running during the meal breaks. Winter working was governed by the available light, starting at 7.30am until 9.30pm. Saturday was an early finish at 5.00pm. Eight or ten days a year were allowed as holidays 'and more if they require them by asking the liberty.' The only punishments were discharge for irregular attendance or disobedience. The mill was powered by a 20hp water wheel and (despite being fed by two rivers) was sometimes stopped by lack of water. There were also periods when the firm was short of work.

They stated the origin of the mill to be 1807, which must be a reference to its rebuilding after the 1806 fire. There is no mention of the firm being woollen manufacturers, that is employing weavers, but the 1834 Pigot's trade directory clearly classifies 'Vickerman, Enoch and Benjamin, and Co. Steps Mill as Merchants and Manufacturers and Joshua Beaumont & Co. of Steps Mill as a Woollen Cloth manufacturer, confirming that they must have been putting out material to handloom weavers who, since they didn't work on the premises, were not included in the questionnaire. It seems that Beaumont and Vickerman still operated as different firms in this field.

The Ten Hour movement to reduce working time for children, led by Richard Oastler, became a popular crusade and there is no doubt that many in the local community, including Steps Mill workers, would have supported it. The campaign was spearheaded by *The Voice of the West Riding,* a newspaper edited and published in Huddersfield by Joshua Hobson which also called for the reform of parliament and trade union rights. It occasionally published lists of subscribers to 'The Victim Fund' to help those who, like Hobson, were persecuted for supporting Radical causes such as freedom of the press. In 1833 a list of Honley supporters includes the name of Abraham Taylor followed by that of Godfrey Oldfield. An Abraham Taylor, aged 37, described as an unmarried clothier, was living at Magwood Bottom in 1841. A decade later the family of his brother-in-law Godfrey Oldfield, a woollen weaver, was living with him. This is too much of a coincidence, especially since Godfrey is not such a common name at this time, and they must have been the subscribers to the *Voice* in 1833 when Abraham was about 30 and Godfrey 28. It was perhaps his sense of injustice which led to an incident resulting in his prosecution in 1840. The road along Magdale had been private for about 60 years and non-tenants had to pay a toll of 3d on their vehicles. On 8th February, George Heaton went through the gate without paying. When he returned he found it locked and the toll keeper refused to let his horse and cart through. Heaton went to fetch Taylor who came with a hammer and smashed the lock and staple from the post. They were fined 6d damages and fines and expenses totalling 23s.6d.[29]

However Taylor was not the only radical in the neighbourhood. After three or four years in the doldrums, radicalism revived with the formation of the Chartist movement in 1838. Its' main paper, *The Northern Star* published lists of 'National Rent' subscribed to finance the organisation's campaign for the Peoples' Charter demanding the reform of parliament. On 16th June, 1839 a donation of 9s. 0d. collected by E. Haigh of Honley from Mag Dale was recorded. The following year money was sent along with a covering letter from the Honley secretary Christopher Wood: 'A few friends to the cause of Chartism and liberty, with an equality of rights and privileges, as free citizens of the world, have sent from Magdale, Honley, the sum of 8s. 6d. to be forwarded to Mr R.J. Richardson, a persecuted Chartist, for speaking and writing the truth.' These amounts are quite impressive when it is remembered that at this time some weavers were only earning an average of 10s a week. When the Chartist leader Henry Vincent visited Honley on the evening of Saturday 23rd October, 1841, he waited outside the Grove Inn while a procession assembled to escort him into the village. On the command 'March', headed by the Honley Chartist flag and a band, around a thousand locals eight abreast made their way under the rising moon to the Socialists' Hall of Science.[30]

Disappointment at the rejection of the Charter, unemployment caused by yet another trade depression, wage cuts and general hostility to industrialisation fuelled widespread unrest culminating in the great strike wave of 1842. In what was subsequently known as the 'plug plot', strikers streamed across the Pennines, forcing local mills to close by letting off the steam from the boilers or emptying the mill dams. Steps Mill was one of those closed, as was Lord's Mill up stream on the Mag and most neighbouring mills and factories. Many locals joined the strikers in marching on Huddersfield where one worker from Lord's Mill was injured in a town centre cavalry charge. The radical sympathies of some Magdalers would no doubt have inclined them to support the strike, even though the Chartist leadership disassociated itself from the movement.

In this climate the employers were apprehensive of the spread of any ideas which could subvert the loyalty of their workforce. In January, 1843 the radical, but anti-Chartist, *Leeds Times* reported:

> *About nine months ago a number of young men at Steps Mill near Huddersfield formed themselves into a society for mental improvement and were making considerable progress. Two or three influential employers of them and their parents, however, have recently suppressed that society by threatening to discharge them if they continued to meet for such purposes any more. No reason has been alleged but that the youths have enough to do to mind their work!! The employers are chiefly Wesleyans of the old school and we suppose they have taken their cue from the late order to petition against national education!*[31]

This certainly alludes to the Vickermans who were from a staunch Methodist family. It would be fascinating to know what inspired these efforts at self-education and who was involved. Thanks to the manufacturers, however, it was nipped in the bud. The small library that had been established was divided among the members.

THE MID NINETEENTH CENTURY

In the author's possession is a small, battered, brown, shiny leather-bound copy of *Wesley's Hymns*. Inside the front cover, in the ornate hand taught at the time, is written [*case and spelling as original*]:

Ann Pogson is my name,
England is my nation
Mag Wood is my dwelling place
and Crist is my salvation
April 30 1837

While at the back is the warning:

Ann Pogson Book
Steal not thiss Book for fear Off shame
for hear you see the Owners Name April 30. 1837

The young woman who owned the new hymn book and proudly inscribed these verses is to be found in the census four years later - Ann Pogson, 20, a cloth birler, living with the family of Jonas Coldwell. She was unmarried but had a daughter, Eliza, aged two. According to the more precise 1851 census Ann was 32, (therefore 18 when she wrote in the book and 20 when she had Eliza) and, still unmarried, was living in the Coldwell house, appropriately at the top of Pogson Lane. Her relationship to this family was not apparent. She had a six-year-old daughter called Sarah, while there is no record of Eliza and we do know whether she was alive or dead. What we can safely assume however, is that Ann had two illegitimate daughters and being from a Methodist background in a small community life could have not been easy for her.

This intimate glimpse into one person's life is a reminder that census returns refer to real people who are not merely names and statistics. This account will therefore try and add some living foliage onto the often bare branches of family trees.[32]

The 1841 census shows 111 males and 103 females, totalling 214 people in 44 dwellings. Unfortunately it does not provide the same detail about birthplace or occupation as later censuses, so its use for analysing one of the important problems of the period – the decline of the handloom weaver and the growth of factory production – is limited.

Power looms did not make great inroads in the local woollen industry until the late 1840s. In fancy weaving competition from power looms took longer to bite and a large proportion of production was still by handloom in the 1860s and 70s. However, for many men it was not a simple case of giving up handloom weaving and getting a job in a mill. A common complaint was that power loom jobs were given to women or girls. Some older handloom weavers would not have been considered suitable for the pace and discipline of factory work, even had they wanted to make the transition.

Thirteen people are listed as clothier in 1841, but by this time it is a vague term referring not only to the small woollen manufacturer who employed others, but also to both the self-employed weaver and the domestic weaver working for a manufacturer. In the first category we know that the clothier David Platt was in fact a manufacturer, since he is entered in the trade directory as such, as are the Donkersley brothers. George Brook, appearing as a clothier in 1841, becomes a woollen power loom weaver in 1851. Clothier, in his case, clearly refers to a hand-loom weaver. His brother Charles, who lived next door at Healdy Butts, is described as a woollen weaver in 1841 and a 'woollen cloth weaver' in 1851.

Magdale, looking eastwards from Magbridge and the dyeworks.

Since he is not referred to specifically as a power loom weaver it seems that, unlike George, he remained at his hand loom. Only four people are denoted woollen weaver, fancy weaver or cloth weaver (the last one, a girl) suggesting that most other 'clothiers' in 1841 were also, more precisely, handloom weavers.

The next main male occupation with eight in the category is cloth dresser, followed by that of slubber and miller, while four women appear as birlers, the main female textile occupation. Although this census does not record juvenile occupations in detail, younger family members may have worked as bobbin winders at home for their parents or in the mill as piecers.

Two men appear as fancy manufacturer, Joseph and Ben Littlewood at Steps, who were both wealthy enough to employ a female servant. Also at Steps, directly overlooking their mill, lived Joshua Beaumont, Enoch Vickerman, who had three female servants, and Benjamin Vickerman - all appearing as woollen manufacturer. Employers and workers therefore lived as immediate neighbours at Magdale and Steps. The physical barriers that later tended to segregate manufacturers from the working classes, as the former moved into mansions and villas in suburbs away from the mills, did not yet exist.

From the Tithe Award of 1847 we have a list of 39 heads of households along with a plan revealing where they lived or, at least, which block of cottages they occupied, enabling us to look at the community in more detail than hitherto. The 1851 census also gives precise names to the locations of these dwellings, helping us to piece together quite a vivid description of the community around this time.

A tour of Steps and Magdale would take us along a road which was still private in 1850. In that year a carter was prosecuted by the toll keeper at Honley Bar for evading payment by driving 'along a private road commencing at Steps Mill and running through property held by Messers Vickerman & Beaumont, under the earl of Dartmouth…' Starting at Steps Bridge, we should take care to cross in daylight and a sober condition since, it was reported by the *Huddersfield Chronicle* in 1853, 'this bridge is a most dangerous one indeed to pass over at night.' It then had no railings and was only a cart-width with a stone parapet a mere one foot to 18 inches high. The drop to the river bed was 'some 18 or 20 feet'. In January of that year a certain 'Dog Ben' Healey, returning home in the dark in a drunken state, fell into the river which was particularly swollen at the time. His remains were not found until the following May in the River Calder near Horbury Bridge.[33]

Having survived the bridge, directly along the right hand side of the road we would see four cottages which later, for reasons now lost, were known as Thimble Street, but were later simply Steps Bridge End. Residents here in 1847 include John Dyson, a cloth miller, Zaccariah Littlewood, a slubber and George Beaumont, a warper. Since John Dyson does not appear in the 1851 census he is probably the Steps Mill man of that name whose funeral is recorded by the *Leeds Mercury* in 1849. He was a member of a friendly society, the Ancient Order of Druids, which, like a working-man's free-masons, provided mutual support for members in crises such as sickness, or, as in this case, funerals. Members from different lodges gathered at the Honley lodge room in the Commercial Inn on Sunday 11th February and formed a procession to Steps Mill. The cortege then moved on to Honley church for a service followed by 'funeral ceremonies peculiar to the order'. There were not only a great number of Druids but, 'The deceased having been an old and faithful servant in the employ of Messrs Beaumont & Co. of Steps Mills, the whole of their adult workman attended the funeral'. The description of him as an 'old' servant does not seem quite apt since he was only in his early 40s.[34]

In 1851, 20 people were living in these four cottages rented from the firm. One family was that of Elliott Kinder, a 48-year-old cloth fuller, with his wife, two sons (aged 21 and 17) who were also cloth millers and three other children. Although he must have worked at Steps Mill he is recorded as employing three men, indicating that he may have worked as a kind of sub-contractor in the milling department, probably employing his own sons. He was also a pig breeding enthusiast and won 15s second prize at the1850 exhibition of the Netherton Association for Improving the Breeds of Pigs and Poultry, in the category for pigs under twelve months old. Whether he kept his pigs in the vicinity of the cottages, as was often the practice, is not recorded. Since the late 1840s there had been a rapid growth of the movement to encourage working men to keep allotments and breed livestock, both on grounds of self improvement and to give them something to fall back on when trade was bad.[35]

A stone's throw up Steps Hill from these cottages was the large house and barn of Steps Farm, the residence of Enoch Vickerman, his wife Elizabeth, 19-year-old daughter Eliza, son John William (at 17 already a bookeeper with the firm) servant, Grace Metcalf, 23 and cook Elizabeth Moorhouse, 27. In 1844 Ben Vickerman had dissolved his partnership with Enoch and Joshua Beaumont and left Steps to take up premises at Taylor Hill. The late 1840s were a time of rapid expansion that saw the building of a steam powered mill with large weaving sheds on a new site on the Honley side of Steps Bridge at what was to become Queens Square. In the 1851 census Enoch Vickerman gave his occupation as 'cloth manufacturer, finisher and merchant' employing 138 males and 155 females – a total of 293 people. Whether all of these worked on the mill premises is not clear. However, it was a large increase on those employed 17 years previously.

Given this large workforce it is surprising that more incidents are not reported, like the one in June 1851 when William Clay, using his foot instead of 'the throwing off handle' to remove the strap of a scribbling machine from the rotating drum became entangled, fracturing his shin bone. Dr Lees, the surgeon who examined him, said many such accidents resulted from carelessness, ignoring the fact that long shifts and tiredness led people to cut corners.[36]

Living at Steps Farm was obviously no handicap to Enoch's status as part of the local elite since Eliza, then 23, married Thomas Brooke of Northgate House, Honley, in September 1854 – the same day as the Battle of Alma, some noted later. The wedding parties met at Steps before forming a procession to Almondbury Church. It was a tragically short marriage. Eliza died a year later in childbirth. Her child, the only son Thomas her husband - later Sir Thomas Brooke - sired, died when he was only 17.[37]

In a cottage, apparently adjoining the farm, there lived Joseph Gledhill, 62, a widower, described as Manager in Woollen Cloth Manufactory. His niece was living in as 'Housekeeper'. Joseph was living in Honley when his son Walter was born in 1821, later moving to Farnley near Leeds, where he was also employed as a mill manager. He settled at Steps in 1846 not long after the death of his wife Jane (nee France). In August the following year he wrote to Walter, who had emigrated to Richland County, Ohio, describing his new position:

> *I am with Vickerman & Beaumont Steps Mill. I have the entire management of the manufacturing. We have ten spinners and 88 powerloomers employing in the weaving factory alone. 116 females and 16 males, so thou may think I have plenty to do. In the scribbling mill there is 11- 60 spindled billeys, and 1 horse of 120 spindles, 21 double stocks of 4 washing machines, and they are carrying on the finishing mill as usual.*

He described the general economic situation with misplaced optimism, since, as we shall see, conditions were to worsen over the following year.

> *The distress in England is rather subsiding as trade is getting a little better, but it is by no means as good as yet, but we have been very fair at our place as yet, very busy in narrow goods, but rather slack in broads. When I say narrows I mean Cassimere's and Doeskins as we make no plains. I know very little of the Mexican War as I do not pay much attention to political matters, but I believe we have more news of the war and sooner here than you have. It is a pity of your Wheat harvest being deficient, it might last. Last year had been very bad for us, but this year we have abundant crops of all grains and most other things.[38]*

There was also a man of the same name, 'night watchman' Joseph Gledhill, living nearby at Steps Fold. Steps Fold and Back Steps Fold are the names given in the 1851 census to the house and four cottages into which the large L-shaped building at Upper Steps Mill was divided.

One dwelling was occupied by David Platt (57) his wife Sarah, unmarried son Thomas (35), two unmarried adult daughters and a female servant, while his son George (33) his wife, (also Sarah), two infant sons and female servant lived in another. Both David and George Platt are described as 'Woollen Manufacturer'. A Thomas Platts [sic] entered in the 1822 *Baines Directory* may be David's father. In 1827 David was running his own business since he was summonsed that year for not taking a town's apprentice. He appears in the Trade Directories, in 1834 and in 1847 as David Platt & Son. That son is apparently George, since Thomas is described in 1851 as 'Clerk in Woollen Manufactory'. This raises the problem of whether the Platts had any manufacturing premises and whether these were now at Upper Steps Mill, since it does not seem that Beaumont & Vickerman were using it.

David's son Thomas, who we know from later references to be Thomas Beaumont Platt, was apparently not even working for his father at this time. A report in the *Leeds*

Mercury for 1850 describes the first 'treat' recorded at Steps Mill, an event which was to become an integral feature of mill life. T.B.Platt is an unusual name and there must be little doubt the same man is referred to:

> *Apraiseworthy addition to the recent festivities in connexion with the factories in this neighbourhood has been made by the liberality of Messers Vickerman & Beaumont. On Thursday evening the 24th of January a tea was provided for all the females and a supper for all the males employed in their extensive establishment. A large room was prepared for the occasion by the skill of the workpeople who hung it tastefully with evergreens, flowers &c. After the removal of the cloth Mr T.B.Platt was called to the chair and Mr F.Vickerman to the vice-chair. The chairman's address was able and appropriate, he urged particularly the importance of unity and the existence of a friendly spirit among the operatives who appeared to concur in the sentiments he uttered and cheered enthusiastically when he resumed his seat. The Rev. T. Benstead of Lockwood was the next speaker and he was warmly received. A splendid brass band and party of glee singers contributed much to the amusement of those present...'*

We will learn about T.B.Platt's subsequent wanderings and tragic fate later.[39]

At Steps Back Fold lived William Mellor, (38) who between 1847 and 1851 had moved from Steps Bridge End. He was a wool carder and both his sons, aged 13 and 14, were described as 'feeder of engine', that is the carding machine they operated with their father. Two daughters were still at school. Two sisters-in-law, one of them with two daughters, were also staying, though from the enumerator's crossings-out William didn't know whether to class them as lodgers or visitors!

The cottages overlooking Steps Fold were described as 'Wood End' and appear in the Tithe Award as one dwelling occupied by Ben Littlewood, fancy manufacturer. By 1851 the head of household was Mary Littlewood (44) who may be Ben's daughter of that name. She was unmarried and employed as a birler. There were two agricultural workers lodging with her, Henry Gibson (30) a farm cartman and George Randerson (21) Farmer, Herdsman and a female visitor, Hannah Senior. It is possible that the house was sub-divided by then since John Owen, a cloth finisher, his wife and daughter are shown living at Wood End, although the enumerator was not sure, writing first 'Fold (back)', then 'Green' before crossing out both.

At the next house Joseph Senior, described in 1841 as an agricultural labourer, then in 1851 as a Stone Delver and a decade later as a stone quarrier, lived with his wife Hannah, manglewoman and son, George Astin, also a stone delver. Her small washhouse, (still referred to as such by locals) survived intact until a few years ago, with its' set-pot boiler and chimney and large vertical slab separating the washing from mangling area. This, along with the two adjacent cottages was known as 'Owlshall'. The first cottage was occupied by William Whitworth (64) Garden Labourer, his wife Martha, 'Oatbread Baker', and son Joseph (26) woollen spinner. In the 1841 census, William is described as a 'fancy weaver' and in 1861 as a 'Woollen hand loom Weaver', hinting that gardening may have been a subsidiary job. William Shaw, 60, described as a 'Woollen Manufacturer', and his wife Hannah, lived in the second cottage. Since he is not recorded as employing anyone, his two sons and daughter, who worked as cloth-dresser, spinner and birler, were probably mill workers and his occupation most likely handloom weaver.

Between Woodend/Owlshall and the upper mill and dam lay Steps Green, which as the name indicates, may have originally been a common open. Here in the 'same house' lived the family of George Mellor (66) described as a 'Woollen Engineer' with, 'or

Set pot in a Magdale wash house.

Manager' added and that of Joseph Newsome a wool slubber – an arrangement that caused the enumerator some confusion. Two Beaumont households, both with young families, were also at Steps Green, headed by George, a woollen spinner and Joseph, a woollen handloom weaver.

Throstlenest was the name of the next cluster of cottages, where slubber Jonathan Roberts lived with his wife, Emma, described as a 'Shoebinder'. Their neighbours were the family of William Haigh a 50 year old bookeeper, accountant and part-time farmer. His brothers Benjamin (husband to Sarah) and Joseph (unmarried), both clothiers in their 40s, had lived next-door a decade before. Like hundreds of other people from the Huddersfield area they left England in the 1840's to build a new life in the United States.

A letter from William and his younger brother, John, a travelling preacher, addressed to them at Canton, Stark County, Ohio survives, giving a wealth of vivid detail about Magdale life in 1848.

> I could record remarkable changes', muses John, ' – scenes-forests, fields, viaducts, railroads, tunnels, telegraphs, preachers, Chapels and many other objects, subjects and things, but you will want to hear of things nearer home, you wish to hear of Magdale and vicinity...

He tells first of the death of old Tom Vickerman on 2nd April. This must be the cloth dresser of that name, recorded aged 50 in the 1841 census. In 1847 he was living at Healdy Butts cottages, where his widow, Sarah, a birler, and unmarried son William, a spinner, continued to live.

The most remarkable local event, however, had been a storm in April 1848 which sent a torrent tearing through fields on Netherton Moor where William farmed, leaving soil 'a foot thick and more on the high road...' It was the worse storm since the Holmfirth flood of 1777, 'There is no Methuselah living can remember or record any such a flood & storm on Netherton Moor', commented John. The weather was more favourable in June when the Haigh's were busy haymaking. 'I & my dear wife have been this day onto the moor – how very verdant fine & fertile fields are brother Williams,' wrote John, 'Rowland & Sydney have been mowing; their father and I cut a few strokes; they first began cutting their grass this afternoon, it is a heavy swathe...' But before all the hay was mown the weather had turned and William, adding his bit to the letter, wrote, 'this day second of July has rained most of the forenoon we expect rainy Harvest all July...'

The most notable change on Magdale was the 'breaking up' of the wood at the back of the houses. Behind the Donkersleys' house it had created an opening so, 'the tenters will be moved back to the rocks' and the wood was cleared as far as Walker Robert's and the Pogson's. 'Wm Whitworth is doing so, at the back of his rocky garden, also making it longer up the wood – they have cut down the plantation by Sutcliffe's fields – it will make a fine field. Indeed Ld. Dartmouth permits them to break up all & ever one of the woods to find work for those ready to starve.'

The economic crisis was making itself felt on Magdale. There had been a strike of powerloom weavers at Steps Mill, who were paid less than others in the neighbourhood, but John didn't think it would achieve anything: 'There has been a great turn out at Steps - another at Dungeon... but what boots it, they must work for little or nothing or clam and starve having nothing...' The domestic weavers were also suffering, 'Richard Crowther is now much reduced has applied to Donkersleys to get some pieces to make, but they are not doing so much trade as they used to say perhaps about two thirds, they did not give him any encouragement'. The Donkersleys were said to have lost £1,500 due to the stoppage of Rawson's bank at Halifax. 'What would our brother Wm do but for his bit of land' queried John, 'Dire distress, doleful ditties might be mentioned, but we wish not to fill our letters with them'. Alliterative passages of the letter read like the lament of an Old Testament prophet, 'trade dull, decaying, dismal, doleful, dying, yea dead – Matthew Beaumont has foolishly left to come starving at Steps: multitudes destitute of employ, food and comforts, numbers dead, many dying…'.

The unemployment and distress had led to a revival of Chartism and a 'great meeting' was held on Castle Hill, which they refer to, although it is not clear whether any of the Haighs attended. They did visit Castle Hill though on a Sunday, when John 'staid at Castlehouses – Mrs H. mounted the hill.' Amid all the gloom they nevertheless enjoyed some domestic happiness. 'Emily knits, her Aunt Haig is teaching her a better way of making a samplar: her Mother Hannah is drudging on from dawn to dark, Garden flowery, flourishing & fruitful…' Emily was eight and her widowed aunt Alice, William's sister-in-law, described in the census as Annuitant, was 58. 'We had much music on Ld's day in the Thorstlenest at the paternal home - Fr [father?] – Bass, Rowland, violin; Rockley Flute; Jono Roberts small fife – Rockley is quite a proficient –arm nearly well [he had broken it]- we are going to Donkersleys to tea'.[40]

There were two households of Donkersleys along Magdale from Throstlenest. The home of the unmarried Donkersley Brothers, Jonas, Timothy and Daniel, aged 50, 42 and 40, each described as 'Woollen Cloth Manufacturer', is called Mag Cottage in the 1851 census. Mary Jagger recounts the story of when, as boys in 1820, her father, John Tilburn, and Daniel were swimming in Steps Mill dam, 'the water at that time was pellucid, and though of great depth, was a favourite bathing place for good swimmers…'. Daniel went under with a cramp and was dragged out unconscious by her father. Both victim and rescuer earned a thrashing from their parents. She refers to the Donkersley's reputation as churchmen and Tories. 'During an election time the three bachelor brothers invariably displayed as flags their blue indigo dyed woollen aprons which old time manufacturers were not too proud to wear.' Their 54-year-old widowed sister Harriott Jessop, and her 27-year-old daughter Sarah, had been living with them since 1841 at least. Their father John, the patriarch of the firm, had died a few years previously in his 70s.[41]

Where the Donkersleys carried out the dyeing is not known, or whether they had their own works of any sort, but in the large field behind their house stood rows of tenters (mentioned in Haigh's letter and shown on the 1854 OS map) used for drying and stretching the cloth after fulling. It would seem most likely that their cloth was fulled at Steps Mill, but where it was then finished is not recorded

The Haighs were on close terms with the family and John writes, 'All the Donkersleys desire kind respects & Mrs Lucy D. especially again this morning with wishing and wondering to know if bror Jo has, or likely to have any increase of family.' Lucy was the wife of John Donkersley, brother of the three bachelors. In 1841, like John Snr, he was recorded as a clothier, but in 1851 he is described simply as a 'Woollen Cloth Maker', and his three brothers as woollen cloth manufacturers. This may only be a difference in terminology, or it may mean that he actually wove cloth himself. Sadly, Lucy, still only in her 40s, died sometime between the summer of 1848 and the 1851 census, leaving John with a daughter, Louisa, the young sons Fenton and John and the eldest Joseph Bedford, described as 'errand boy', who lived with his bachelor uncles.

The dwelling next to John Donkersley was occupied by Abraham Taylor and his brother in law, Godfrey Oldfield and family, whom we met in the 1830's. These houses at the top of Healdy Butts Lane were also occupied by the families of Walter Beaumont, a wool dyer; Sam Horne, a farm labourer, born at Gunthwaite Hall, and his two sons (also agricultural workers) and Joseph Brook, a 'woollen cloth milner', who lived with Joseph France, a 'Woollen Fancy Hand Loom Weaver'.

How such small cottages housed, in this case, six people and at least one handloom, plus all its gear and utensils, is amazing. Accounts of people sleeping alongside the loom, or in the loft space, must reflect a common condition. The actual weaving was only part of the process. The weft had to be wound onto bobbins which were soaked then 'wuzzed', swung round in a container to remove the surplus water, before being put in the shuttles. Warps required sizing - treating with a gluey, foul smelling substance to make them taunt – they could often be seen stretched out on hedges or walls to dry. They then had to be beamed and 'reached in' to the loom. If a fancy pattern was being woven with the aid of a Jacquard machine this could be a complex procedure. The clatter of the handloom would have been a familiar sound all along Magdale.

In the 1851 Census Healdy/Yealde Butts must have sounded so foreign to the enumerator that it becomes transformed into 'Yell-de-butts'! Here there were five cottages, three of them inhabited by families of Brooks, totalling 21 persons, headed by brothers Charles (56) (great-great-great-great grandfather of the author), George (53) and Charles' son Mark (33). Mark was a slubber, George a power loom weaver and Charles simply a 'woollen cloth weaver' which, as we have seen, indicates a handloom weaver. The widow of Tom Vickerman lived at Healdy Butts, with her son William aged 27, a woollen spinner. Her eldest son, Charles, had left home a few years previously to work for the Tolsons of Dalton, where he rose to be manager of the spinning department. (He also later worked in this capacity for Mrs Fairburn of Mirfield, one of the few woman woollen manufacturers, who ran Farnley Mill). The last cottage was occupied by Joseph Horn, a wool dyer, his wife, a birler, and six children from two to 15, the eldest, Elizabeth, working as a piecer.

Ascending Pogson's Lane there was the house of Walker Roberts, also a woollen cloth weaver, now aged 70. His unmarried son, George, 39, was specified as a woollen hand loom weaver'. John Haigh referred to the breaking up of the wood behind his house and Pogson's. We met Ann Pogson at the opening of this chapter and so can move on to Magbridge. Walter Garside, a wool dyer, lived here and although we can't say for sure where he worked, the fact that two other wool dyers, Abraham Marsden and Walter Taylor lived at Magbridge (and one at Healdy Butts) would seem to be related to the proximity of the large Farrar's dyeworks on the Honley side of the river, described below. Walter Taylor, 40, was a widower and the Haighs, relaying gossip about who is getting wed, comments casually, 'Walter Taylor Mag brig (son of late Jam Taylor) was spurned…'.

Abraham Sutcliffe (62) a farmer of 13 acres lived with his wife, four children and grand-daughter (a decade previously there had been ten people in the household). It would have been difficult to make a living from 13 acres so he was fortunate having four other wage earners in the family, Jonathan who was a stone mason, Abraham, a wool sorter, and Emma and his grand daughter Elizabeth, both power loom weavers. Abraham had been farming at Magbridge at least since 1835 when, according to the *Leeds Mercury*, in an act of 'wanton cruelty', one of his cows was mutilated in an axe attack. As we have seen from the Haigh letter in 1848 he had cleared a new field. A farm labourer, Henry Bingley, also lived at Magbridge, but we can't assume he worked for Abraham. A 64-year-old widowed farm labourer, Frederic France, and his son, a fancy weaver, also lived in the same house as Bingley.

Magdale from the west.

Joshua Beaumont memorial (*left*) in Honley graveyard
alongside that of Magdalen his wife (*right*).

HAND LOOM TO FACTORY

The most visible sign of industrial change in the late 1840s was the construction of the railway embankment, almost 100 foot high at its centre, connecting the cutting from Robin Hood Tunnel to that at Timinets, just before Honley station. A wide tunnel was built beneath the embankment to allow access to the coal pits at Wood Top (through what are now called the Cockatoo Fields). Work on the Penistone line was underway in 1846, when at least four men died working on the Thurstonland tunnel alone. Before its contours were softened by the growth of vegetation the embankment of fresh earth must have scarred the landscape and dominated Steps. Honley station opened in 1850 integrating the locality more closely with the national economy.

The strides in industrialisation were celebrated the following year by the Great Exhibition at Crystal Palace. Vickerman & Beaumont were among the local firms exhibiting their manufactures, listed as black 'broad cloths, cassimeres and doeskins, piece dyed, permanent colour and finish.' Some of the employees may have had the opportunity to visit the exhibition on one of the cheap railway excursions that were laid on, seeing London for the first time.

With the expansion of the railways, the annual trip also became a popular mill tradition, as well as the annual treat. Breaks from the routine of work caused great excitement and provided the highlight of many people's year. Often they were reported in the local press. Treats and trips helped foster gratitude and loyalty to the employer and reinforce the feeling that workers were part of one big family firm, in the same way that the country aristocracy paternalistically regarded their estate workers. By jointly celebrating patriotic events loyalty to Queen and Country was also encouraged.

In January 1855 the Steps Mill treat was held at the Coach & Horses, when 'the time was spent in interesting discussions on the war and other things connected therewith.' Vickerman & Beaumont had encouraged their workers to support the 'Patriotic Fund' for the relief of dependents of troops in the Crimea and a list of about 60 individual subscribers, plus collective contributions from woolsorters, knotters, burlers and powerloom weavers, was published in the *Examiner*. On 29th April the following year another treat at the George and Dragon was held to celebrate the peace.[42]

In the early 1860s the majority of weavers in the Huddersfield area, especially in the fancy trade, were still handloom weavers working at home. However, the old way of life of domestic production was being steadily eroded by expansion of the factory system. One consequence of this was the decline of population in many handloom weaving areas, as people moved to urban centres where more reliable and better paid work was to be found. Even between 1841 and 1851 there was a fall in the number of people in Magdale from around 214 to 199 - but over the following decades it declined further to 187 in 1861, 178 in 1871 and 175 in 1881. The main reduction was among males.

In the 1861 census, Enoch Vickerman is described as a woollen manufacturer employing 120 males and 222 females, a total of 342 - an increase of 49 since 1851, or around 16%. However male workers had in fact declined from 138. One explanation of this is evident in the report of a treat for 200 female operatives of Joshua Beaumont & Co in the 'large' birling room at Queens Square in 1868. The *Examiner* reported that, the mill was fully employed, despite a trade depression, and that all the power looms at Steps factory were attended by females.[43]

Enoch Vickerman died in October 1861 at Harrogate, 'the large manufactory with which the deceased was connected being closed for the day', to mark his funeral. The other senior partner, Joshua Beaumont, along with Magdalen his wife, was temporarily away from his residence Parkton Grove during the 1861 census, since he is recorded as the absent head of household. His 22-year-old son George, now described as a woollen cloth manufacturer, and 25 year old daughter, Magdalen, were at home along with a cook and housemaid. Joshua died in 1866 and was buried near the north wall of Honley cemetery, where his wife Magdalen was buried alongside him 21 years later beneath a beautiful Celtic cross. As we shall see, his eldest son, Alfred, took over the running of the firm.[44]

The increased use of female labour is one obvious reason for the decline of men in textile occupations. Steps Mills did not determine the labour market though. At a time when it was not unusual to walk two or three miles to work, employment could be found in more than half a dozen other mills within only a mile or so of Magdale, including the large factory of the John Brookes at Armitage Bridge which did employ male weavers.

In 1851 there were at least six male handloom weavers on Magdale and a further five men simply described as 'weavers' who most probably also worked a hand loom. There was only one specified male power loom weaver. By 1861 this had risen to four. The number of female power loom weavers however remained constant at seven. By 1871 the contrast is stark. Although the census uses only the general term 'woollen weaver', 11 of these are females and eight are men. But five of the latter were those described as hand-loom weavers in the 1861 census and the likelihood of them getting a factory power loom weaving job at their ages, when even younger men were not being set on, is remote. Two of these aged hand loom weavers were Abraham Taylor and Godfrey Oldfield, now aged 67 and 75, Abraham still unmarried, Godfrey now widowed and described as unemployed.

In 1861 David Platt described himself as a 'Woollen Cloth Manufacturer - Employs 28 men & 4 women'. This would imply that they worked on the premises, since the Donkersley brothers, also woollen manufacturers but employing only out-workers, do not specify a number of employees. At this time Platt does not have any sons living nearby and it is not clear who was involved with the firm. However, by December 1866, when the dissolution is announced of the partnership between David and his son Thomas Beaumont Platt, woollen manufacturers of Steps Mill, it is clear their premises were at the upper mill. Perhaps the firm dissolved due to David's retirement since he was now turned 70. In the 1871 census only Thomas is down as Woollen Manufacture, David senior possibly having died.

Intriguingly, the birthplace of Thomas's 13-year-old son, David, is given as Australia and that of his wife, Agnis, as Liverpool, accounting for his absence in the years around 1860. He had four other children and employed a nurse born in Cheshire. In 1872 it was announced he was leaving Steps Mill and most of his belongings were advertised for sale, including all the drawing room and dining room furniture in mahogany, the contents of four bedrooms, 'kitchen requisites' and a dinner service, as well framed engravings and about 100 books. Although now 55 he apparently still hankered for a more adventurous life, since his destination was Iowa. There, on 27th February, 1875, while walking home along a railway line one winter's night, he collapsed and was run over by a train. He was sufficiently well regarded for this distant tragedy to warrant a report in the *Examiner*.[45]

Another firm whose passing marked a break with the old days of domestic clothiers was that of the Donkersleys. By 1869 Fenton, aged 30 (down as a woollen manufacturer in the 1861 census) was running the business, since in that year he prosecuted Humphrey Mellor of Netherton for obtaining goods under false pretences. Messrs Donkersley are described as having a cloth warehouse (whether in the locality, or at Huddersfield is not revealed) where Mellor came for suit lengths of black broadcloth and tweed which he claimed, untruthfully, his father would pay for. Jonas died in 1872, aged 75, and in the 1881 census Timothy appears as a retired woollen manufacturer and his nephew, Joseph Bedford Donkersley, as a woollen merchant. Timothy died in 1887 aged 81 and Joseph Bedford, who was only 52, two years later. John Bentley Donkersley died in 1901 aged 58.[46]

THE GROVE INN

The Grove Inn was built in a former quarry below the old steep turnpike road over Hangingstone, facing onto what is now the main road that sweeps round the valley side to Berry Brow. This route, which became the new turnpike road, was probably constructed shortly after 1833, when the carriage drive of Parkton Grove House, which joins Hangingstone Road, is described as still opening onto the turnpike, along which the London coach passed twice a day. In the 1841 census Honley born John Sanderson appears at Grove as a 'beerseller'. By 1843 the pub is described as the Grove House Inn at Park Grove, when, tenanted by John Sanderson, it appeared among the lots in the sale of the estate of Timothy Bentley's Lockwood Brewery. A stable and shed was attached and later photos show a building very like the surviving Jacob's Well at Honley.

Sanderson remained the tenant eight years later when, on 26th December, 1850, he and his wife, Harriet, laid on a tea party, 'prepared after first rate fashion by the worthy hostess' for 40 burlers from Steps Mill, followed by singing and dancing. The following month he hosted an 'excellent and very substantial supper' for 30 unspecified employees from the mill. In the 1851 census he is described as an innkeeper, rather than beer seller. That same year his 13-year-old daughter, Agnes, was acclaimed for her needlework when she stitched in silk a two-foot square sampler depicting the counties and county towns of England and Wales.[47]

As well as mill treats, the Grove was the venue for another popular working class recreation. Honley Harriers, under the huntsman Samuel Norcliffe, met there in 1856. The chase began in the immediate vicinity when a hare, or 'puss' as the animal was often referred to, was set up in Hangingstones Wood. After vainly trying to swim the river Holme it led the dogs up the steep hillside towards Castle Hill earning itself time for a brief respite at Farnley Hey, before doubling back down Park Lane. This time it successfully crossed the river Holme and climbed the steep wooded valley with the hounds in close pursuit, over Netherton Moor to Scar Top and back through Spring Wood. Again it crossed the river, pausing to shake itself dry as the hounds closed in. Norcliffe, seemingly moved by the animal's resilience and satisfied by the chase, called them off. 'Thus ended one of the best hare hunts held in this locality'.[48]

The pub continued to be associated with the hunt since, in 1868, 'friends of the chase' attended the funeral of landlord William Broadbent at Honley, along with 'a very large number of people', including members of the Independent Order of Odd Fellows who carried the coffin. They may have had a meeting room at the Grove. William's widow, Betty, took over the pub and by 1881 it was being run by his son, Amos. He was also a 'brother' in a 'secret' friendly society, the United Order of Free Gardeners – Adam's Past Lodge, which in May 1879 held its monthly meeting and supper at the Grove.[49]

On a dark January evening in 1859 Police Constable Robert Wardle, based at Parkgate, Berry Brow, heard two men acting suspiciously in the wood off the 'Upper Road' (the old Turnpike) behind the Grove. He climbed over the wall to investigate, but was thrown bodily by one of the men into the old quarry – a drop of over eight yards onto a pile of

Mary Elizabeth Sykes, her husband Luke Noble Sykes and an unknown
woman (possibly their servant Sarah Asquith) outside the Grove
Inn. The photograph was taken between 1905 and 1917.

A tramcar on service No. 10 to Honley Bridge, passes the Grove
Inn. The pub supplied Bentley and Shaw's Town Ales.

stones. Two workers returning home from Armitage Bridge Mill heard groaning and having located him with a light obtained from the inn, carried the PC into the building. A surgeon was brought from Honley and Wardle was taken home to Parkgate and next morning to Huddersfield Infirmary, where he was treated for a broken elbow and thigh. The case was treated as attempted murder, but no one appears to have been prosecuted.[50]

Until the 1890s it was the usual practice to hold inquests in pubs and at least one was held at the Grove Inn. On the morning of Sunday, 21st July, 1861 'great excitement was caused at Steps Mills and throughout the neighbourhood when a body was seen on the river bed at Steps Bridge. PC Edward Antrobus was brought from Honley and the dead man was found to be John Crosfields, a 58-year-old dye-house labourer who lived at Steps with his wife, Sarah, son Richard, a cloth dresser, and a three-year-old grandson. It was presumed that, returning at night from work at Huddersfield and only 100 yards from home, he had fallen over the parapet of 'this very dangerous bridge'. At the inquest William Horne said he had been with the deceased at the Grove from 10 pm until closing time and had shook hands and parted with him at the end of Steps Lane. Ben Heaton described finding the body, which was lying on a dry part of the river bed about 20 feet below, the deceased's head and face 'were much crushed.' The jury found that it was an accidental death and 'a long and desultory discussion' took place about the danger, since this was the third fatality there. The bridge was only six feet wide and the parapets only 18 inches high, and it was thought the tenants of the mill ought to make it safe for the hundreds of their workpeople who passed back and forth every day. It was, the jury agreed, 'a disgrace to the place.'[51]

1862-1871 POLICE INCIDENTS AND ACCIDENTS

Perhaps the most exciting event in the vicinity of Magdale since the 'Plug Riots' 20 years before also involved PC Antrobus. He had made himself so detestable to people in Honley by throwing his weight around that, on the evening of 23rd June 1862, they tried to lynch him. A stone-throwing crowd of over 200, shouting 'Kill the bugger', chased him from near the church, down the fields and over the Mag footbridge almost to Steps Mill, where he was stunned by blow. He was temporarily saved by two men, including Josiah France, a Honley woollen designer, who we will meet again later. The crowd thought Antrobus was faking his injury and gave chase again over Steps Bridge. He sought refuge with PC Wardle at Parkgate and accompanied by the PC and a police sergeant, returned home later that evening to the macabre sight of his effigy being burned. The three were stoned by the crowd and had to seek refuge in the Jacob's Well. Public opinion sided with the 'rioters', a committee was set up to defend the dozens summonsed over the incident and even the *Examiner* thought Antrobus had overstepped the mark. The 'respectable' inhabitants of Honley also successfully petitioned for his removal and, according to the Chief Constable, Antrobus was glad to go.[52]

PC Yates of Netherton was indirectly affected by an incident on 12th November, 1863, when his 11-year-old daughter Harriett was the victim of an attempted rape while on her way home along the 'lonely road between Steps Mill and Netherton', after taking dinner to a worker at the mill. Two witnesses, Grace Mellor, who was also going to the mill with dinners, and a boy, W B Brook, saw the suspect, identified as Joseph Heap of Scholes, in 'Steps Wood'. Although Heap had previously assaulted a girl near Scholes he was sentenced by Holmfirth magistrates to only three months hard labour.[53]

A more unusual crime reached the courts in 1868. On 5th December, 1867 a beehive belonging to William Broadbent of Magbridge disappeared. Suspicion fell on Tom Taylor of Honley and when PC Morely visited his house the hive was discovered.

Taylor's excuse was that he had 'found' it, although it had been on Broadbent's property. This was not as trivial as it seems, since the hive contained 30lbs of honey valued at 1s a pound, a total equivalent to a week's wage or more for many people at that time.[54]

Several tragedies are recorded on Magdale during this decade. In 1865 the four-year-old daughter of woolsorter Abraham Mallinson and his wife Elizabeth was burnt to death trying to take a potato from a pan on the fire, where they were boiling to feed the pigs. The following year the hand of an unnamed young woman was badly shattered firing a pistol on bonfire night. (This custom, as well as the use of fireworks, frequently led to injuries - a girl in Honley was shot in the head the same evening). In 1867 weaver Walter Beaumont's wife, 44-year-old Harriet, a victim of fits, received a fatal head injury after falling down stairs at home.

Nine-year-old Allen Drake was almost drowned on Shrove Tuesday 1868 while playing with some other boys on the temporary wooden weir on the River Holme which had replaced the 'damstones', swept away in the flood earlier that year. He fell in the river, which was swollen after rain and was fished out near Steps Bridge, (referred to as the 'Bow bridge' in the *Examiner* report), and taken into the wool drying stove at Steps Mill to recover. Emma Green, aged five, the daughter of cloth dresser Allen Green, was less lucky when she fell into Steps Mill dam in 1871. One of the mill workers, George Brook, jumped in and pulled her out, but she was already dead. An accident is recorded in Steps Mill in June 1868 when a 14-year-old girl piecer from Berry Brow 'narrowly escaped being crushed to death' when trapped between a self-acting mule and a pillar.[55]

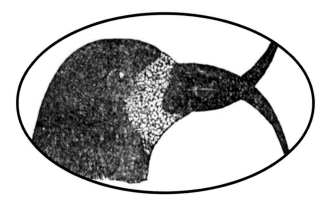

Seth Mosley's drawing of a freak cross billed rook in Alfred Beaumont's collection.

STEPS MILL AND BEAUMONT'S BIRDS

The 1881 census shows a continued decrease in the number of males in textile occupations. Ten men (a quarter of those in textile jobs) were working as weavers and it is safe to assume that by now most if not all of them were operating power looms - especially as worsted weaver was a recently established branch of trade. In its report on the state of trade at the close of 1878 the *Examiner* alluded to the increased number of worsted manufacturers and the fact that in the Huddersfield area, medium and best quality goods were 'brought to the greatest perfection [and] are now being manufactured almost exclusively in this district...'.[56]

Thirteen out of 21 females in textile jobs were also weavers, five of them worsted. There also appears one Overlooker in Worsted mill and one Clerk in Worsted Manufactory. The former is Robert Booth, who had already worked for Joshua Beaumont's for almost 30 years and continued until his death in 1893. However, 1881 was the year that control of this firm, now headed by Joshua Beaumont's eldest son Alfred, changed hands.

Of all the inhabitants of Steps and Magdale in the 19th century, Alfred is the one on whom we have the most biographical detail and who was best known among his contemporaries. He is absent from the 1841 census at Steps where his parents and brother George were then living and from Parkton Grove in both 1851 and 1861. In October 1858, he was living at Park Cottage, Yew Green, when he married Mary, the daughter of Eleanor and Joseph Hirst, a wealthy Meltham woollen manufacturer and merchant employing 350 people. She died in childbirth eight months later and her grief stricken parents built the picturesque Wilshaw church as a memorial. Alfred attended its consecration on 27th April, 1863. He remained close to the family and was the chief mourner at his former mother-in-law's funeral in 1881.[57]

Alfred, now described as woollen manufacturer of Greave (near Wilshaw) acted as a prover of his father's will in October 1866 and took over both the firm and the family home. By October 1867, when he appears as one of the grandly titled, but obsolete, grand jurors of the Court Leet of the Manor of Huddersfield, his address is given as Steps Mill. At Parkton Grove in 1871, then aged 39, he was living with his second wife, Dublin born Deborah Selina (24). A visitor, Harriet Colley, described as a merchant, also from Dublin, may have been an in-law.[58]

Alfred appears to have been a popular, if typically paternalistic, employer. In January the following year he and his wife attended the work peoples' New Year treat held in a 'neatly decorated' room at Steps Mill. Honley Brass Band provided the musical accompaniment of 'God Bless the Prince of Wales' and other tunes. One of the employees, James Beaumont, proposed the health of Mr and Mrs Beaumont while John Gledhill conveyed thanks for stopping the mill at one o'clock on Saturdays 'and hoped that the workpeople would return the kindness by increased diligence and care'. Alfred 'spoke on the good feeling which ought to subsist between masters and workmen, especially between foremen and those under them...he should always be ready to make any reasonable concession which would be of real advantage to the work hands'. The following year after tea in the burling room, a deputation of six workpeople went to Parkton Grove to present Mrs Beaumont with a set of flower and fruit stands 'as a token of their respect and esteem'.[59]

As a boy Alfred had attended a preparatory school at Storthes Hall run by the multi-talented Peter Inchbald, who inspired a generation of local naturalists. The pupils explored the woods and fields round about and Alfred was one of those who developed a life-long passion for collecting specimens of birds and insects. Many of his birds

Alfred Beaumont (*left upper*) and his wife Mary (*left lower*) as seen in Wilshaw Church.
Wishaw Church, (*right*) built in memory of Alfred Beaumont's late wife, Mary.

were stuffed by a famous local taxidermist, James Reid Mosley of Almondbury Bank, father of Seth Lister Mosley, later a well-known naturalist, author of many books and articles, including the 1915 *Birds of the Huddersfield District*, and, in 1920, the first curator of the Tolson Memorial Museum at Ravensknowle. Seth recollected how as a boy he accompanied his father to Beaumont's Yew Green residence to 'case up' the bird collection. His own interest in nature was encouraged by Mr Beaumont 'giving me some of his duplicate insects and books'. Occasionally, Alfred would visit the Mosleys' house at Almondbury Bank to see how work was progressing on particular birds.[60]

To start his collection Seth was also given the eggs of a pair of crows shot by the gamekeeper in Storthes Hall wood and sent by Beaumont to his father for stuffing. Beaumont also collected freaks, such as a rook with a cross-bill shot at Taylor Hill and a pure white whinchat. He shot some of his own specimens, including a merlin bagged on Slaithwaite moor where he had shooting rights. His view of birds was, to say the least, unsentimental. Mosley records that ring ouzels were formerly common on the moor but Beaumont 'shot a great many of them as they set the grouse up by their alarm note...' In August 1878 Lord Dartmouth and his daughters accompanied him on a shoot where 17½ brace of grouse were bagged. For a time he also had shooting rights on Crosland Moor where the game included the common partridge and in Brooke's wood at Armitage Bridge. He was a 'well built and strong active man,' and would sometimes keep watch along with the gamekeepers. One night he apprehended a poacher and took his gun, telling him if he wanted to avoid prosecution he had to pay a shilling a week for twelve weeks. When the man had dutifully paid all the instalments, Alfred gave him back his gun and the money, with a warning not to do it again.[61]

Other species in the collection, now unknown in the district and rare even then, included a hobby shot at Castle Hill and a bittern from Armitage Bridge. The latter was stuffed by another Almondbury Bank taxidermist, John Gough. Among the foreign species was an Eskimo Curlew, an American bird which was extinct by the early 20th century. Alfred also had a collection of mammals and, since it was not known to contain a wild cat, Mosley concluded that the one Mrs Jagger recorded in her *History of Honley* as trapped and killed by Alfred and his gamekeeper must have been a feral feline.[62]

Eighty cases of British birds from his collection were loaned for the 1860 Annual Conversazione of the Huddersfield Literary and Scientific Society (HLSS). Some appeared in the Huddersfield Naturalists Society's (HNS) exhibitions at the Philosophical Hall in 1862 and the Gymnasium Hall in 1864, where he delivered talks on ornithology and lepidoptera. He also exhibited several cases of birds at the Honley Industrial Exhibition held in the National School in September 1866. Alfred increased his collection by buying some cases from another of J.R. Mosley's clients, the collector John Burgess of Brighouse, who ran Seed Hill dyeworks.[63]

Unfortunately, some of Beaumont's birds turned out not to be what they seemed. Indeed his friend, and writer of his obituary, the prominent local naturalist George Taylor Porritt, stated indignantly that, although bought 'on good authority', some rare specimens were 'fraudulently imposed upon him', including a White's Thrush, supposedly killed at Almondbury Bank in 1864, an Andalusian Hemipode (a quail-like native of southern Spain and north Africa), reputedly caught in a field at Hillhouse in April 1865 and a Ross' Gull.

Alfred was a both a member and a vice-president of the HLSS and served as a president and patron of HNS in 1865 and 1866. At the HNS exhibition in October 1866 he 'created quite a sensation' by inviting Paul du Chaillu, the famous French-American explorer and the first European to see and describe the gorilla. He gave two lectures on his expeditions in West Africa, chaired by Beaumont, who introduced him saying, 'their kind friend had kindly consented, after refusing many other towns, to visit the most distinguished town of Huddersfield.' How they became acquainted is not recorded, but they were close enough for Monsieur du Chaillu to be invited to stay at Beaumont's residence. Unfortunately, at this time, Beaumont appears to have still been living at Greave, so Steps narrowly misses the acclaim of hosting this famous visitor.[64]

Enthusiasm for natural history and collecting bridged class barriers which in other spheres were well demarcated. Beaumont's night watchman at Steps Mill, James Jessop was, along with Henry Wright, one of the founders of Honley Naturalists Society in 1875. Wright had his own collection of Lepidoptera, which he donated to Ravensknowle in 1920. Seth Mosley, with obvious empathy, described how a sparkle came into old Henry's eyes when he relived the capture of his favourite specimen, 'Ah! That Puss Moth were a great 'un when I fun it. It wor pearked on Alfred Beaumont's garden wall one mornin' when I wor goin' to me wark at six o'clock. An' I took it an' kept it I me bobbin box while neet as ah came hoam. It war a grand un'. [65]

Queens Square Mill. Handloom weavers trying out new patterns before being put into full production by power loom (1950s).

One gets the impression that Alfred's own passion for collecting took precedence over running the family firm! This may partly account for the fact that on 5th March, 1881 it was announced in the *Huddersfield Chronicle*:

> *'HEAVY FAILURE ... Yesterday afternoon a petition was filed in Huddersfield County Court for the liquidation of the affairs of Alfred Beaumont, Steps Mill, Honley and Greenwood's Yard, Huddersfield, woollen manufacturer and merchant trading under the style or firm of Joshua Beaumont and Company. The liabilities are stated at £65,000...'*

He was also apparently heavily mortgaged, having bought the mill, farm and other properties at Steps from the Dartmouth estate in 1874. On 21st May an advert appeared for the sale of the stock and implements of Steps Farm, followed by adverts for mill machinery and Parkton Grove house, the entire contents of which were auctioned in July. They included a drawing room suite in 'walnut wood, richly upholstered' and dining room furniture in pollarded oak. Amongst the household effects were advertised 'an extensive collection of Cured Birds of various species, moths etc together with a costly library of books...' which were moved to Huddersfield to be sold. The moths numbered about 15,000 including 'very rare and valuable specimens'. Among the 500 or so volumes was *Birds of Great Britain* by John Gould, valued for its beautiful lithographs. The lots were put on show at the post office buildings in Northumberland Street and auctioned by George Tinker on 10th August.[66]

The bird collection of 295 cases, described as 'a unique collection of great variety... in the best state of preservation' was bought for £200 on behalf of the HLSS by Major Graham, Samuel Learoyd and C.P. Hobkirk. Two years later 274 specimens, including golden and sea-eagles and other already rare birds, were exhibited in a 'Fine Arts and

Industrial Exhibition' at Huddersfield Technical School and Mechanics Institute on Queen Street. The catalogue explained that, 'These were the property of Mr Alfred Beaumont and were purchased for the purpose of forming the nucleus of a Town's Museum'. After the exhibition closed they were briefly put on show at the Technical School until the space was needed for classrooms. Here they languished in storage, or the corridors, until a Museum was opened in 1901 in the new wing of the Technical College with Mosley employed as part time curator. Limited public access was allowed from 1905 but they were used mainly as a teaching collection.

They were transferred with the rest of the specimens to the new Ravensknowle Museum in 1920, where Mosley was primarily responsible for organising the new bird room that opened in 1925. He frequently referred to the importance of the nucleus provided by Beaumont's collection and his own long association with it.[67] Alfred's insect collection was lost to the district when it was bought by a London dealer and broken up - a constant source of regret to Seth Mosley when setting up Ravensknowle Museum, since many of the species in it were no longer to be found locally. Alfred began a second collection of birds after he left the district for Lewisham around 1884.[68]

Parkton Grove house was sold in October 1881, described as a Valuable Leasehold family residence with gardens, stables, carriage house etc, situated at Steps, Honley in a 'well sheltered and choice situation, commanding extensive views of the district'. The auctioneers mentioned the proximity of the railway station as a selling point - but failed to point out that the railway line ran only a few yards above the house, on a steep embankment along which goods and passenger trains clattered more frequently than they do today. The house still looks over what is left of Steps Mill, a reminder of the source of the wealth that allowed Alfred the leisure and the money to accumulate his collection. A remnant of that collection survives, re-cased, re-mounted and a little faded, in the bird room of the Tolson Museum - a monument to Parkton Grove, Alfred Beaumont and his contribution to the study of natural history.[69]

JOSIAH'S – QUEENS SQUARE MILL

Machinery auctioned at Steps Mill in 1881 included scribblers, self-acting mules and power looms although it is not explicit whether this was from the Lower mill or from Queens Square. However it appears that this was the time that Queen Square was taken over by Josiah France. In 1861 Josiah, aged 29, lived at Well Hill in Honley. Already a widower, he was living with his widowed mother, his sister Ann and his son Ben and daughter Penelope. His occupation was given as 'woollen pattern designer', but this was for his late father's firm, Benjamin France and Sons. A decade later his elder brother, Ben, also a widower, was living with the family. His occupation was described as 'former cloth manufacturer', while Josiah's hds become that of 'woollen cloth manufacturer, employing 160 hands'. His son Ben was a manufacturer's apprentice. They occupied premises in Thirstin Mill.

In 1878 he had rented room and power at Neiley Mills and in April of that year advertised for a tuner for Hutchinson & Hollingworth looms. Three years later he wanted pattern weavers, promising 'constant employment' indicating that his business was thriving. According to the 1881 Trade Directory he was a woollen manufacturer, but he may already have been involved in worsted production. It seems that when he took over Queens Square Mill in 1881, it was as a going concern and that Joshua Beaumont & Co. were already manufacturing worsted, since, as we have seen, one of their employees, Robert Booth, is described that year as 'overlooker in a worsted factory'.

Queens Square Mill in the foreground with both Upper Steps (*right*) and Reins Mill (*left*) visible.

Within two years Josiah was caught up in the great Huddersfield weavers' strike/lock-out which began in early March 1883, as a result of the employers' attempt to impose a new pay scale. He wrote to the *Examiner* of 17th March listing the prices he was offering for the weaving of 13 different types of goods, including white worsted, (for which he said he had been paying more than other employers), thin fancies, heavy fancies and mixtures. His address is given as 'Steps Mill, Honley'. There must have been considerable hardship among his weavers who did not return to work until 7th May and who together only received a total of £29 7s. strike pay. Despite this, Josiah was apparently respected by both workers and employers since during an 1891 court case between Larchfield Mills and some women menders over damage to a worsted piece, 'It was ultimately agreed that the matter should be referred to Mr Josiah France as umpire...', to decide whether it was bad workmanship or poor material at fault.[70]

Josiah also bought Parkton Grove where he was recorded in the 1891 census as a worsted cloth manufacturer aged 59. His sister Ann, then 57, (who died three years later) was still living with him along with a cook and housekeeper. His daughter Penelope had married Dr D. Winder in April 1888 - an occasion celebrated by the whole mill. The engine was stopped at 12.30 and the workpeople gathered in the mending room. The cashier, Charles Burley, presided, while the chief designer, Fred Moseley, presented the newlyweds with a dining table centre piece and booklet listing the names of the subscribers. In September 1888 Penelope and her new spouse joined a Queens Square Mill trip to Scarborough. On this occasion, as usual, some trippers missed the return train – one was left behind twice when he left the later train for a drink at Normanton.[71]

Two years later the destination was Southport. The train left Honley at 5.15 am for the three-hour journey. On arrival, some were then dismayed to find that they still had a half mile walk from the shore to find the sea. After visiting the marine lake, botanical gardens and winter gardens and enjoying carriage and donkey rides, they, 'being Honleyites, soon longed for the time when they might feast their eyes on their native valley'. This most of them did by 11.30pm. apart from one man who arrived at the station to see the trip train steaming off from another platform. By a combination of trains he got within walking distance, arriving home exhausted in the early hours, with 'the advantage and consolation of looking back upon a journey certainly unique, [he] has inwardly decided not to take again'. Some of the trippers may have brought back a souvenir they hadn't bargained on.

A few weeks later the nuisance inspector for South Crosland Local Board reported two cases of scarlet fever which he believed had originated in Southport. The Board medical officer was instructed to contact his counterpart in Southport to trace the source of the contagion.[72]

STEPS MILLS – LOWER AND UPPER

Ownership of Steps Mill and neighbouring land and property apparently passed from Alfred Beaumont to Thomas Brooke in 1881 and it was under the latter's name that plans were passed for a new weaving shed and enlarged boiler house. The firm of Joshuah Beaumont & Co. was salvaged after Alfred's bankruptcy to continue woollen manufacture at the mill under new management, primarily the Dysons of Netherton. In 1887, the firm held a treat at the Oddfellows' Hall in Netherton to mark the coming of age of Arthur Dyson. He appears in the 1894 trade directory as a woollen manufacturere of the firm Joshua Beaumont & Co.

The continuity of Joshua Beaumont & Co was marked in the career of Robert Booth, who, on his death in 1893, had served the firm for 40 years. Born in 1822, he was the son of John Booth of Scholes, a Wesleyan preacher. He appears in the 1861 census at Steps, along with his wife Martha, seven children and mother-in-law Sarah Hawkyard, working as an 'Overlooker in Woollen Factory'. His cottage at Steps was advertised to let in 1870 but, if he moved at all, it wasn't many doors away. In 1871 he is recorded as a 'Woollen Manufacturers Bookeeper', but a decade later as 'Overlooker in Worsted mill', indicating that the firm had now changed production. He is again entered as 'Book keeper' in 1891, apparently a responsibility combined with overlooker. A Congregationalist and teetotaller, his glowing obituary described him as 'a man so thoroughly upright, so genial and so kindly in all the various relations of life...the very incarnation of trustworthiness... His pleasures were of the simplest purest character. He was fond of books and was also an ardent lover of nature, especially delighting in long walks through the beautiful scenery of his native county and in visiting ancient buildings...' Apparently it was a sudden death since an old friend wrote;

> For him life's thread, so brittle broke
> The way he always deemed was best,
> The way he wished, one sudden stroke-
> One pang, and then – eternal rest.

The fact that the *Examiner* carried an obituary and that the workpeople of Joshua Beaumont & Co. sent two wreaths, indicates the esteem in which he was held.[73]

While Robert lived most of his adult life at Steps, his son, Clarkson, made up for his father's lack of geographical mobility. In 1861, aged 14, he was working as a woollen mule piecer. By 1881 he had become a traveller, that is a salesman for a firm, and was again living at Steps with his wife Eliza and son Robbie Davies Booth, whose birth place is given as Rushville United States of America. Whether his work had taken him to the States, we don't know. In 1891 Robert Jnr, now 21, was living with his grandfather Robert and working as a wool dyer.

Upper Steps Mill at the right of the picture and the cottages of Magdale behind.

Upper Steps Mill (*left*) and Steps Mill (*right*), at the height of their operation.

UPPER STEPS MILL

What was happening at Upper Steps Mill and who occupied it after Thomas Platt left in 1872 is obscure until 1885. By then it was occupied by Ben Donkersley and his brother William, cloth finishers. They were a different branch of the 'Donks' to those on Magdale, their father being John Donkersley of Lower Thirstin. Ben became a Wesleyan Methodist Sunday School scholar in 1832, later becoming a teacher himself, then a superintendent and, in 1856, a fully accredited preacher. By 1868 they had premises in the Moll mill. In 1873 their eight-year-old niece was killed nearby when their driver lost control of the horse and their cart crashed down the banking on the Old Moll Road. They may have moved to Upper Steps Mill shortly after this since there is no mention of them again at the Moll mill.[74]

Ben and William were clearly not good judges of horses. In 1885 they needed a horse 'to draw loads of coals and bring pieces from the low mill up the hill to the upper mill'. They bought one for £28 from George Dyson, an innkeeper of Dock Street, Huddersfield, who said it would easily pull a ton-and-a-half of coal up the hill 'before they could say Jack Robinson'. Taking his word and declining his offer of a written warranty, they took the horse but, at its first attempt to draw eight hundredweight of pieces, it 'jibbed' at the bottom of the hill. Complaining to Dyson, he said it was not actually his horse but he had sold it on behalf of Tom Jenkinson a cab proprietor of Marsh. A vet brought in by the Donkersleys confirmed that it was indeed 'a jibber'. It only fetched £12.17s.6d at auction and since they had spent £3.10s feeding it for 7 weeks, they took a claim to the County Court of breach of warranty for losses of £18.12s.6d. When they told the Judge it had stopped at the hill, he remarked, evidently amused by their gullibility, 'Perhaps it was waiting for you to say Jack Robinson?' Since they didn't have a warranty and had not examined the horse properly it was declared a clear case of caveat emptor and costs were awarded to the defendants.

Two years later Ben retired and, in December 1887, it was advertised that since the firm was giving up Upper Steps Mill their finishing machinery was to be sold. They had by now a new horse, Polly, a dark brown seven-year-old mare, 15-2 hands high, which was also auctioned.[75]

As for the 'Donks o't'Dale', their passing marked a break with the old days of domestic clothiers. By 1869 Fenton, aged 30 (down as a woollen manufacturer in the 1861 census), was running the business, since in that year he prosecuted Humphrey Mellor of Netherton for obtaining goods under false pretences. Messers Donkersley are described as having a cloth warehouse, (whether in the locality, or at Huddersfield is not revealed), where Mellor came for black broadcloth and tweed suit lengths which he promised his father would pay for. Jonas died in 1872, aged 75, and in the 1881 census Timothy appears as a retired woollen manufacturer and his nephew, Joseph Bedford Donkersley, as a woollen merchant. Timothy died in 1887 aged 81 and Joseph Bedford died two years later aged only 52, the last male member of the family remaining on Magdale.[76]

MAGBRIDGE DYEWORKS

Another Magdale occupation was that of dyer. In 1851 there had been four described as such, three of them living at Magbridge. In 1881 three men were in the census as blue dyer and by the following decade, six. It is likely that some, if not all, of these worked at the dyeworks at Magbridge on the Honley side of the river. In 1796 a lease from the Dartmouth estate refers to the dyehouse of Joseph Robinson and in 1805 to a dyehouse and waterwheel. Robinson was involved in a protracted water-rights dispute with the

Magdale dyeworks boilerhouse.

The break up
of the Magdale
dyeworks boilers
during demolition
in the 1980s.

trustees of Clitheroe School who owned adjacent land. In 1847 the dyeworks was advertised for sale, along with another at Smithy Place. It was later acquired by George William and Thomas Farrar. Mary Jagger describes them as 'men of open-handed generosity and unfailing cheerfulness ... celebrated for their fine horses as for their good dyeing'. They were both also 'robust Conservatives' and 'devoted churchmen'.[77]

In 1861 they installed a new boiler from Arnolds of Huddersfield at the cost of £205. This may have been when the steam engine was first being installed. At the 1866 Pollution of Rivers Enquiry at Huddersfield, G.W. Farrar said he employed 26 hands and dyed both cloth and wool and produced blue and black colours, using about a chest and a half of indigo a year – a chest averaging nearly 400lbs. The sediment from the effluent settling tanks was put on the land. Ashes from the steam engine were used for road mending and the remainder dumped in the river.[78]

By 1871 the workforce had increased to 35. In 1876 Farrar Bros workers along with those of Gledhill & Roberts, bobbin makers of Neiley Mill, were treated to a trip to Hull via Goole.[79]

However, in February 1886, Farrar Bros of Thirstin Dyeworks (as it was then described) were declared bankrupt and their farm stock advertised for sale. Further disaster struck. In October a fire was spotted at the works by Edward Taylor of Magdale shortly before midnight. A bucket chain was organised but 33 pieces worth £1000 were destroyed. It was said that to have been caused by overheating of drying cloth. Although they were insured, at their creditors meeting in 1892, it was claimed they had sustained a serious loss from the fire, and that, along with bad trade and a steep rise in the price of coal, had contributed to their predicament.

That year Lower Thirstin Dyeworks, was sold along with a 20 hp horizontal steam engine (22 inch cylinder, 28 inch stroke, 10 foot fly wheel) by James Kilburn of Meltham, an Arnold and a Horsfield boiler, respectively 26 and 28 foot long, 7 foot 6 inch diameter, plus 6 1/2 acres of land adjoining the works under Spring Wood, as well as G.W. Farrar's residence at Cliffe House with its pleasure grounds, flower and fruit gardens, two summer houses and green house at the bottom of Green Cliff. The business was purchased by William Schofield & Lupton Littlewood, (G. W. Farrar's brother in law), from W. H. Armitage the trustee, and then leased back to the Farrars for rent of £330 per annum. In April Schofield and Littlewood found themselves in court for the 12s in the pound they had promised to creditors when they bought the bankrupts' assets. The firm managed to continue as Farrar & Co. indigo, wool and cloth dyers.[80]

OLD MOLL MILL

A number of silk dyers also lived on Magdale. In 1881 there were two and a decade later four. These undoubtedly worked at Moll Springs Mill, then on a private road, occupied as a silk dyeworks by George W. Oldham since 1866. Extensive rebuilding of the former mill on the site had taken place and 70 guests, including the contractors, attended the opening. Other manufacturers also operated on the premises. In 1871 the workforce in the silk dyeing business was only 13, compared to 37 woollen workers and 14 cloth finishers. Oldham (originally from Derby and his wife Eliza from the silk town of Macclesfield), who had been in Honley since May 1857, now lived at Clitheroe above the mill, where they also farmed 14 acres. He and his son, George Thompson Oldham, rapidly expanded the new business, according to Mrs Jagger, overcoming 'a world of difficulties' and, it seems, not always by observing the law. In 1888 they were found in breach of the factory act by working 14-, 15- and 16-year-old boys excessive hours.[81]

Reins Mill (*right*) and the cottages at Reins with Northgate farm in the middle distance
and the white-painted wooden Hebble bridge and Magdale dam in the foreground.

Upper Steps Mill (*centre*) with Parkton Grove in the middle distance
and Queens Square Mill (*right*) in another early photograph.

The family residence by 1891 was at The Stubbings, a large house at the Netherton end of Spring Wood bottom. Although Liberals active in local politics, in 1902 they drew the line at municipal involvement when it came to paying rates towards Honley UDC's electric lighting scheme, since their works already produced its own supply, and was hailed as the first silk dyers in the country to do so. Fifty years of the firm was celebrated along with G.W. Oldham's 77th birthday in 1907, when the workpeople presented him with a silver rose bowl. Relations with the workers were not always so harmonious. During the wave of industrial militancy just before the war about 50 of their dyers joined the union and 100 successfully came out on strike for a wage increase. On his death in 1914, aged 84, G.W.Oldham was hailed as a pioneer of silk dyeing.

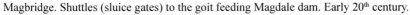

The Stubbings, home of George William Oldham in Magdale and (*inset*) George William.

Magbridge. Shuttles (sluice gates) to the goit feeding Magdale dam. Early 20th century.

Magdale Fields in the 1970s.

Magdale from Sentry.

RURAL MAGDALE

FARMING

Manufacturers like Beaumont, Farrar and Oldham often combined farming with their business, but the declining importance of agriculture during the second half of the century is reflected in the reduction of farming occupations mentioned in the census. At the beginning of the 1800's, as we have seen, both Steps farm and Healdy Butts farm are recorded. References to the latter disappear, but land continued to be farmed at Magbridge. One field, behind the Magbridge cottages, has now been reclaimed by woodland. In 1851 seven agricultural occupations are recorded – two farm cartmen, a herdsman, a cowherd and three farm labourers – as well as a farmer, Abraham Sutcliffe at Magbridge, and a part time farmer, William Haigh. Abraham Sutcliffe's land is recorded as 13 acres and William Haigh's as 14 acres. From the Haigh's letters to America we know that much of this was on Netherton Moor and included six separate pieces of mowing grass, pasture, three lots of potatoes, two of turnips, sweet clover, Italian ryegrass, lints, oats, barley, parsnips, mangel wurzel, mazlin, rye and winter and spring wheat.

Enoch Vickerman's Steps farm, then 25 acres, employed three labourers in 1861. Whether these were the three recorded as living on Magdale - Sam Horn, (aged 72) his son, Henry (30) and James Jessop – is not apparent , although Jessop was later also employed at Steps Mill as a watchman. Sam, who in the 1820's had been a cropper, was quite elderly for such a rigorous outdoor occupation and perhaps his death in October 1863, following a 12-day bout of pneumonia, was related to his work.[82]

1871 saw the arrival of the first steam thresher in Honley marking the strides which were being made in farm mechanisation. In this year we find Abraham Sutcliffe's son William, at Magbridge, reduced to eleven acres. William Ashmore, 47 and Henry Brook, 41, are recorded as agricultural labourers. Henry subsequently became a dry-stone waller and mason, building, or repairing, many of the walls which have now fallen into such dilapidation, especially on Netherton Moor.

A decade later, on 25th May, 1881, the sale of Steps farm, following the bankruptcy of Joshua Beaumont & Co, helps build a picture of the typical equipment and stock on a farm of this size. It included three powerful draught horses, a stack of hay, waggon, spring lurry, roller, harrows, ploughs, American rake, potato scuffler, Bentall's scarifier, horse hay rake, grass mowing machine, grass spreading machine, hay chopper, corn crusher, cake crusher, winnowing machine, turnip drill, and sets of gears for shafts and plough. Among the livestock were poultry, eight milch cows and heifers and 16 sheep. The latter at least were pastured on Netherton Moor since in January the flock, then numbering 20, had been worried by dogs and one killed and partly eaten. A separate auction on 15th July shows us the location of standing crops, 'hay grass, oats and after grass in land lately occupied by Mr Alfred Beaumont, situate at Netherton Moor, Mag Bridge and Steps Mill. Sale commences Far Hay. Close 3.30pm'.[83]

At this time Henry Moore, 56, is recorded as a farmer living at Steps, along with his son Tom, 20, an agricultural labourer. He may have been managing the farm for Beaumont. Nearby lived Thomas Simpson, aged 28, described simply as 'farmers man', and his wife. He remains there a decade later - still a 'farmers man'.

By now Steps farm was occupied by James Lancaster, 75, a farmer who had moved from Thurstonland with his wife, 22 years his junior, and five children, two of whom

Spring Wood.

were millworkers. He is probably the Thurstonland farmer of that name whose cattle suffered an outbreak of foot and mouth disease in 1883. The early 1880s were a bad time for farmers not only because of this epidemic, but also due to a general slump in agricultural prices.

James Jessop, who we met in 1861 as a farm labourer, is recorded in the 1871 and 1881 censuses as a night-watchman. We know this was at Steps Mill since in 1878 he was called as a witness in the case of poachers trespassing on the railway embankment in search of rabbits. He was a keen naturalist and with his friend Henry Wright was one of the founders of Honley Naturalist Society. He moved from Honley to Magdale about 1860 where a baby was added to the family of six children, most bearing unusual names. Henry Wright was attributed with naming three ancient beech trees at the bottom of Spring Wood 'the three sisters' after Jessop's eldest daughters Angelina, Anaminta and Domina. His wife Tamor died in 1875 and only his youngest unmarried daughters Armenal and Hannah, both worsted weavers, remained at home. Possibly with the departure of Alfred Beaumont he lost his night-watchman's job, since by 1883 he was reliant solely on farming, but on what land we don't know. He was summonsed that year for not maintaining his two grandchildren. Which daughter was involved is not recorded, but she was apparently unmarried and in no position to keep them herself since James said he had often helped her out. James complained he only had eight acres and a few cows and would be better off earning 12s a week as a farm labourer, 'He was persecuted to death almost and he had no means of keeping himself'. When a shilling a week maintenance order was imposed, he replied, 'Well, then they'll ha to take me for it'. A year later he probably felt even more persecuted when he received a letter from the South Crosland Local Board ordering him to repair one of his fences. [84]

WOODS AND WELLS

The woodland which became Spring Wood originally covered Netherton Moor, but much was cleared even before the enclosure of the common land in 1788 when the boundaries of Dartmouth's land was demarcated. Under the enclosure act the freeholders lost the right to cut wood or take stone from Mag Spring. Once predominantly oak woodland much is now birch following successive fires, but a few older trees remain, especially the two large beeches (the remnant, as we have seen above, of The Three Sisters) near the spring at Magbridge. Although the spring is a notable feature, the name may not be derived from this, but from the method of harvesting the young wood, which was sold to be cut by the buyer. An advert for Magwood, Spring Wood appeared in the *Leeds Mercury* in 1814, 'for sale 60 oak and other trees and 1,861 poles; trees and poles marked with red and white paint to be left standing.' As part of the Manor of Honley it came under the jurisdiction of the relic of feudal times, the Court Baron, which in 1853, meeting at the Coach & Horses, Honley, discussed repair of the way through it. This was apparently wide enough to take carts, since the previous year George Kaye was prosecuted for damaging a fence belonging to Dartmouth while driving through the wood to Netherton. In 1854 the overlooker of the estate woods, Mr Mellor, was returning from his rounds of Farnley Tyas when he saw a great blaze in Spring Wood. The locals organised to fight it but 5 or 6 acres were damaged. This 'Terrible Conflagration', as it was dubbed by the *Huddersfield Examiner,* was supposed to be the work of an 'incendiary'. A less serious fire in 1868, the origin of which was a mystery, destroyed only half an acre when it was beaten out by locals and police constables.[85]

Dartmouth was also keen to protect the wood against poachers, although there was no preserved game to be shot. Robert Hobson, the landlord of the Black Bull at Berry Brow and a friend, were prosecuted in December 1870 for trespassing in pursuit of game. They were seen by Alfred Beaumont ranging the wood with a setter and a pointer while Hobson carried a double-barrelled shotgun. Hobson claimed that they were just looking for their young dog which had run off into the wood as they were passing by. They called on Beaumont in the evening and asked him not to report them, but when he refused Hobson was said to have bragged he had always shot in the wood and would continue to do so. He had a previous conviction for a similar offence and was fined 20s plus 12s costs.[86]

Although the wood had been damaged by fire and was harvested commercially the local ecology was healthy enough to support a diverse range of species. G. T. Porritt, nationally renowned for his work on moths, particularly melanistic (dark) varieties, caught a number of specimens in Spring Wood, including, in 1887, one from which he bred a perfectly melanic Mottled Beauty (Boarmia repandata), different from any previously known in the area, and two years later the rare Pine Beauty (Trachea piniperda). He apparently enjoyed the area so much he came to live at Crosland Hall around 1894 and remained there for a decade.[87]

Spring Wood was also the last refuge of some sensitive species like the common snake and blindworm, a legless lizard also known as the slow worm, Anguis fragilis. In 1870 a man repairing the wood wall near Lord's Mill found a snake 18 inches long and another about the same length was killed the following year. They were said to still be common in the wood. Mary Jagger also remembers when she was a child, a snake 'of considerable length was killed in Spring-wood' while Seth Mosley reported in 1914 that many older Honley residents recollected snakes 'in meadows at Magdale'. The Newsome naturalist W.E.L Wattam had a blind worm brought to him in July 1904 from Spring Wood and while walking there in June 1913, he saw two others.[88]

Nan Hob well.

The woods of Magdale inspired the superstitious as well as the scientific mind. Spring Wood and Nan Hob Wood were both believed to be among the last refuges of fairies. Most of this folklore has been lost, but belief in Fairies, Boggarts and Will o'the Wisps was certainly alive in the late nineteenth century. A poem published in 1875 depicts them still haunting the glade around the spring.

> Thy witches are gone, but the fairy-folks good,
> Yet frolic 'tis said, in the Nook of Springwood,
> And dance to the fountain-fall's moon mellowed glee,
> Around the charmed trunk of the twin beechen tree.

The spring was used for human consumption well into the 20th century and for livestock up to the 1980s, when it became too unreliable and polluted. A love poem printed in 1883 describes the scene as a young woman drinks water from the spring. In the poet's imagination she becomes Hebe, the cup-bearer to the gods.

> As in the margin of Spring Wood,
> The moss illumined fountain nigh,
> The Lily of Mag Valley stood,
> Watching the pearl drops as they gushed,
> From the rock casket cool and bright,
> And down amongst the flowerets rushed,
> Chanting the praise of freedoms light.

Below the wood known to locals by the same name and near the bank of the Holme, Steps also has its own spring, Nan Hob, which flows from the same strata as that in Spring Wood. This name is of mysterious origin, both elements being associated with fairies, and expresses the enchanted atmosphere of the place. There is a carved stone trough to channel the water and the steep banking above the spring is retained by a wall of dressed masonry. It is possible that it was the ancient object of veneration since Mrs Jagger notes that in living memory people made a 'pilgrimage' to the well on Mayday to drink its restorative waters. The tradition she may have been alluding to was going strong in the 1860s, although, by then, on the second Sunday of May as recorded on this occasion in 1868:

> *MAY MORNING – The Honley Brass Band paid their annual visit to the Nan Hob Spring on Sunday morning last. About five hundred persons also visited the spring on the morning in question, a majority of whom took a hearty draught of pure water, which is constantly and unceasingly gushing from the mountain side. For a couple of hours the band performed a selection of music, while the visitors promenaded on the adjacent grounds. It is in contemplation to invite a number of neighbouring bands on the next occasion and should nothing arise to prevent this arrangement being carried out, a very large gathering may be expected on the second Sunday in May next year. [89]*

The Magdale poem also refers to the spring's legendary properties.

> *'Thy stories of marvellous agencies still,*
> *I hear with delight and mystical thrill,*
> *For though science may scout the hour was divine,*
> *When the spring of Nan-hob and her neighbours ran wine...*

The springs might not have run with wine, but they were vital water sources. In 1868, in response to 'complaints as to the scarcity of water at Steps Mills, Far Reins and that locality', some inhabitants began digging at the foot of the hill at Far Reins until a stream of 'pure soft water' gushed out. A well of stone and flags was built supplying water 'sufficient for the domestic purposes of the whole neighbourhood'.[90]

A complaint about the state of the road to Nan Hobb spring was made at the 1853 Court Baron, which instructed that a notice be posted on the church door ordering the Honley stone merchants, Brown and Bower, who had a stone works near the bottom of Gynn Lane, to make safe the road, 'which they have made dangerous by opening a quarry there.' The remains of the quarry are still to be seen and may have been the 'fairy like spot' where the 1887 Jubilee was celebrated. Since the account of the event in the *Examiner* was obviously written by a participant, or someone closely acquainted with Magdale, it is worth quoting in full.

MAGDALE JUBILEE CELEBRATIONS

> *They can have jubilees anywhere but here; there's nivver nowt in't' Dale like other spots'. So said one neighbour to another and it got to the ears of one who takes a great interest in all that concerns Magdale and its inhabitants. He said, ' But you shall hae one, lass, an' it shall be a ripper'. A few of the male portion of the inhabitants formed themselves into a committee, with Mr Joseph Whitworth as chairman, met at Amos Broadbent's, determined to have a jubilee celebration and fixed the date for July 16th. It was decided also to have a substantial tea and if possible to have it in the lovely and fairy like spot called Shady Bower, in the wood behind Nan Hob. A deputation waited upon Colonel Brooke, the owner of the wood, who very kindly gave his permission. The preparations went on apace. Messrs Joshua Beaumont and Josiah France kindly lent tables and forms, which the young men carried up to the wood (no easy task) and, after tea carried back again. The place was beautifully decorated, and the royal standard floated in the breeze. Four o'clock was fixed for the tea, but just before that time some very long faces were pulled. There had been no arrangement made with the clerk of the weather, and there came on a thunderstorm with heavy rain; but after a while it cleared up a little and the people, young and old assembled to the tune of two hundred. Some of the old dames had to be helped up the hill, and seemed very well pleased with the attention, one or two remarking, that there were, 'Noan so young as they used to be,' or they could,' hae com'd up as weel as ony on yo.' Previous to the children who had their tea first commencing a verse of 'God Save the Queen,' was sung. When the young ones had enjoyed the good things provided, their places were speedily filled as the weather looked threatening, and*

all had their teas before the rain came on again. Every one was delighted with the tea, many saying they 'nivver sat de'an to a better tea in their lauves.' Unfortunately, the after part of the proceedings had to be abandoned, owing to the rain. A field had been taken for the sports, and a string band engaged for dancing, and many were looking forward to spending a pleasant evening. As far as it went it was a very pleasant evening indeed, and had it not been for the rain the affair would have been a great success. there was not a wrong word said, nor a hitch in the whole proceedings. Mr Jonathan Roberts of Park Gate, provided the tea, and it reflected the greatest credit on him for the manner in which it was served.[91]

Nan Hob Wood and well were evidently popular locations – in fact too popular, as described in *Country Rambles*, published in the *Huddersfield Echo* of 9th July, 1887.

Nan Hob Well is uniquely situated. Its retreat is most picturesque, and its sylvan shades are very charming. I knew that on this occasion, the burning sun was flaming overhead, but so protected was this grotto, by the open leaves of the oak, the ash and the horse chestnut and the sycamore, that his piercing rays could not pierce it. Here the "fern's green fronds enwrapped the rocks", and "mosses green revealed their nests," while, "charming songsters filled the air", and "frisking lambs the woodlands roved".

The writer was captivated by a frog he found, but soon his reverie was interrupted, first by 'a band of irreverent School Board educated youths' and then:

two or three neatly-clad damsels approached, filled their cans with water and hastened away just as a band of ruffians came up, and with oaths, betting language and indecent gestures turned what was a moment before, a peaceful and solitary retreat, into a pandemonium where nought but man was vile. As I left I felt I should have been delighted to have seen the backs of these men laid bare and the cat used mercilessly on them.'

The vicinity attracted local artists as well as ruffians. One of the pictures shown in the Huddersfield Art Society exhibition in 1897 by S. Wright of Newtown, Honley, was of 'The River Holme near Nan Hobb'. [92]

A naturalist, writing in the *Examiner* in 1904 under the name Hedera Helix (Ivy), described Nan Hob Wood as 'a place having the peculiar advantage of being 'easy of access, but somewhat secluded...' He recorded some of the moths found there, including the Pale Brindled Beauty and Dotted Border, as well as noting a large excrescence known as a 'witch knot' on one of the Scots Pines. Referred to as Mag Wood, this area was, along with Spring Wood, studied by T. W. Woodhead of Huddersfield Technical College, a founder in 1904 of the Committee for Survey and Study of British Vegetation, (later the British Ecological Society), as part of his survey of woodland plants. His findings were published in the *Linnean Society Journal* in 1906.

INTO THE TWENTIETH CENTURY

From a low of 167 in 1891 the population showed an increase to 181 in 1901. The number of dwellings increased from 43 to 47, but whether this was due to new building, or subdivision of properties, we don't know. In 1890 a plan by J B Donkersley was not passed due to the house 'not having sufficient air space.' 'Hillside' was built 1897/98 and it may be the large modernised house advertised to let on Magdale in 1900, along with four acres of land, but its location is not specified. It had three large bedrooms, a large bedroom and bathroom combined, a water closet, dining room, breakfast room and kitchen and was described as 15 minutes from the tram or train. Another house that year on Magdale was advertised at an annual rent of £15, but again we do not know where it was since the named occupant does not appear in the census. Housing and environmental conditions were improved by the changes in local government, which by the end of the century had emerged in its recognisably modern form with elected representatives and committees. In 1876 the Local Government Board (LB) for South Crosland was established, abolishing the powers of the old Township and Maglordship bodies. John Bedford Donkersley was one of the first representatives to be elected by the ratepayers. Under the 1894 Local Government Act the more democratic South Crosland Urban District Council took over administration of Magdale's highways, water and sanitation in 1895.[93]

In 1881 much of the former Dartmouth estate at the Steps end of Magdale passed to Thomas Brooke of Armitage Bridge mills. On the 1891 census, Maglordship, as the name of the hamlet, is crossed out, indicating that someone realised the term was now long obsolete following the abolition of the manorial court and the disposal of much Dartmouth land. However, when Wood Cottage was advertised for sale in 1904 the ground rent was still payable to the Earl of Dartmouth at £10 per annum under a lease from 1882.

PRIVIES

In 1887 the Local Board ordered J. B. Donkersely to go ahead with approved plans for new privies and the following year it passed plans submitted by the executors of B. Boothroyd, Magdale for two more privies. These would probably still be earth closets since it was not until 1892 South Crosland Local Board negotiated with its Honley counterpart to build a sewage works to take effluent from Magdale. The land at Armitage Bridge was provided by Colonel Brooke and he and the South Crosland Local Board stipulated that the sewage works should be of sufficient capacity to take Magdale sewage.

Most of the dwellings continued to have earth 'long drop' privies and the disposal of effluent from water closets could be unsanitary even by the standards of the time. In 1892 a letter was sent to the Local Board from Joshua Beaumont & Co., complaining about the water closet of Mr Ellis emptying into Steps Mill dam. A notice was sent ordering him to provide a cesspool. Ellis lived at Wood Cottage, the Donkersley's former residence, which, in May of that year was advertised to let 'containing large sitting room, two kitchens on ground floor, four bedrooms and large bathroom, wc, keeping cellar in basement, hot and cold water throughout; with two acres of land attached, south aspect – Apply to Thomas Kaye, Honley.' Two months later John Ellis wrote to the LB from Blackpool, stating that he had taken away the water closet from his property at Wood Cottage. The new tenant must have been left using the earth closet.

The nuisance inspector reported defective drainage at the house of Henry Hinchliffe at Steps in 1894 and the clerk to the Local Board was instructed to notify Mr Whitworth, agent of landlord Thomas Brooke, to rectify it. In 1897 there was a problem with rain water running into the privies of H. Jenkinson and others, while two years later farmers, accustomed to lead their cattle from Netherton Moor to use the well at Magbridge, complained that it had been 'broken into' by a sewer causing 'great inconvenience'. Abbey & Hanson, the UDC's contractors, were ordered in 1901 to replace the walled drain under the house of Sam Beaumont at Magbridge by pipes, covered with six inches of concrete and to put in sewers connecting the four houses at Steps occupied by Mrs James Thewlis and others. Despite these improvements in sanitation and drainage, many dwellings continued with outside earth closets until after World War II.[84]

Outbreaks of disease, particularly those dangerous to children, were common. There was a scarlet fever outbreak in 1895, resulting in the houses of Joseph Donkersley and Robert Noble being fumigated by the nuisance inspector. In the hot summer of August 1901 there was another outbreak, with three cases attended to by Dr Smailes of Honley, the UDC's medical officer, in the same house at Steps. He reported,

> This house was in a very dirty condition and after it had been stoved by the inspector he would advise the council to order it to be cleaned and limewashed before being occupied as he understood the family was leaving. Three houses at the river side were in a very unhealthy lot and were not really fit to be inhabited; they were below the road, got no sunshine and had no through ventilation. At this place he had received several complaints of offensive effluvia coming from the Steps Mill dam. Owing to the scarcity of water in the river the mud had been constantly uncovered and caused a great nuisance.

The UDC had also to complain to Joshua Beaumont & Co. about 'the offensive state' of Magdale dam in July 1903 during another heat wave; 'The water was run off and an extensive surface of decomposing mud left exposed in the hot rays of the sun'. Apparently the dam had been drained, since Upper Steps Mill was still empty at this time following an unsuccessful attempt to lease it in 1901.

The residents of Magdale were not doing all they could to improve sanitation. In February 1898 the UDC wrote to the owner of Thorstlenest, asking him to ensure that tenants put their ashes in the place provided and three months later the nuisance inspector reported that, 'the tenants at Magdale had thrown domestic refuse into the goit and the river. He had requested all the tenants to discontinue this practice and they promised to do so'. [95]

Pollution of rivers was a growing concern. As late as 1870 the Mag was clean enough to support leeches, although the fact that this was thought interesting enough to report to the *Examiner* perhaps shows it was not the norm and the species involved was one with a high tolerance of pollution. Under the 1876 River Pollution Act Local Authorities were authorised to give facilities to manufacturers to carry off effluent so long as it was not a nuisance to the district. Prior to 1886 dye water went directly into Mag Brook via Thirstin Dyke from Eastwood's Thirstin Mill until the mill drain was connected to the Honley Local Board sewer. But many mills continued to discharge into the river and up to the end of the 1970s it often flowed different colours, or covered in foam.[96]

As we have seen, at the 1866 Pollution of Rivers Enquiry at Huddersfield, G. W. Farrar of Thirstin Dyeworks thought it alright to mention that ashes from the boiler house were dumped in the river, but in 1894 South Crosland Local Board sent a letter to his successor Robert Farrar complaining about ashes polluting the stream.[97]

BRIDGES

In 1863, 18 months after John Crosfield fell into the river from Steps Bridge, someone under the name 'M' wrote to the *Huddersfield Chronicle* complaining that it was still 'dangerous to cross it either by day or by night' and he knew of one person who would only attempt it at night on his hands and knees! Only 'a feeble attempt' had been made to improve it at one end. He pointed out that Vickerman and Beaumont had extensive mills on both sides of the bridge, one wall of which directly abutted onto it. The *Chronicle* commented that the foreman of the inquest jury, James Wrigley, had tried to ascertain who was responsible for the bridge and had contacted both Mr Vickerman and Mr Thynne, Lord Dartmouth's agent. It was 'a monument of disgrace to the owner, a disgrace to the occupiers and a continual source of danger to all who have to pass over it'.

The following week, in a letter entitled 'The Celebrated Bridge at Honley', 'NO NAME' of Steps rebutted 'M', claiming that the feeble improvements included replacing a low, rotten rail by three-foot boarding and placing a gas lamp which burnt from sunset to sunrise. This provoked a further response from the *Chronicle* correspondent. The improvements had only been made at one end of the bridge by the firm, but this was an admission they were responsible for making all the bridge safe. Furthermore, 'There was no "public road" at all about Steps nor in Magdale, until a few years ago, before then, there used to be a bar or gate across the road at Steps beyond which no vehicle could go without permission'. Magdale was then an 'occupation road' and not repaired by any public authority. John Robinson had first insisted on the right of way for access to his dye works at Thirstin and since then others had done the same until it had been opened up to the public. James Wrigley, at the last inquest, had said that Netherton ratepayers only repaired the road to the bottom of Steps Hill, not right up to the bridge, while Honley denied any responsibility for the hundred yards or so from the bridge to the turnpike road at Reins, therefore this stretch was still an occupation road as far as Lower Steps Mill. He concluded about the bridge, 'It was much regretted at the time that it was not swept away amongst others by the Holmfirth Flood'.[98]

On 19th March G. W. Farrar of the Thirstin dyeworks reported to a Honley ratepayers' meeting that he and others had met with James Wrigley and corresponded with Lord Dartmouth about the problem. It was agreed, 'after a good deal of discussion', that Honley and Netherton townships take joint public responsibility for the bridge and the roads at each end.[99]

Metal railings were put on the parapet at some stage and joint repairs were agreed in September 1881. In June 1893 Steps Bridge was once more of concern, when the South Crosland LB agreed to join with Honley LB in altering the rails. Honley LB considered the railings to be in a 'dangerous condition.' and consented to the repairs. At the same time it was agreed to raise the wall on Mag Bridge and to widen it on the NW side.[100]

Another vital bridge was the footbridge leading up Steps Fields to Honley village. In the 19th century this was referred to as the Hebble Bridge a term dating back at least to the 1500s denoting a 'narrow bridge'. A small bridge appears on the 1829 oil painting of Steps but when it was first built is not recorded. It is not mentioned at the time of a severe thunder storm on 20th April, 1822 when a cloudburst over Meltham and Holmfirth;

sent down by the two channels of those valleys an immense flood of water the streams of which came into contact at a place called Steps. The effect was truly tremendous and highly alarmed all the neighbourhood. A breast of water from seven to nine feet high rushed down the valley and spread its desolation along its course but happily no lives as far as we have heard were lost.'

The Mag Dyke flooded again during a storm in November 1866 rendering Mag Bridge impassable. On 1st February, 1868 there was an even more ferocious flood which damaged the Steps Mill 'damstones' (weir) and eroded three yards of the river bank towards the dam. The wooden Hebble Bridge, connecting Honley and South Crosland at the bottom of Steps Fields, was washed away, the wreckage coming to rest two miles away at Lockwood. The townships agreed to replace it and a new wooden one, designed for 20s by Mr. Blakeley of Netherton, and built by Edward Holdroyd of Honley for £16, was in place by the beginning of April. This can be seen on an early photo of Steps Mill and Reins.[101]

In 1893, Joshua Beaumont & Co wrote to the Local Board about the state of another footbridge across the Upper Mill dam. In response the local board clerk instructed the firm the following year to 'protect the bridge over the goit at the back of the mill', which must refer to the same one. The firm replied that 'They were not aware of any danger near their mill' and put in a counter complaint about the very bad state of road at Upper Steps Mill, 'suggesting a remedy for flooding to which their mill is at present subject.' This footbridge, where the dam narrows to enter the wheel race, fell into disrepair after Josiah France closed in the 1970s and has not been replaced.[102]

Honley UDC met a deputation from South Crosland UDC in August 1899 to discuss the repair of joint bridges including the Hebble bridge at Steps, which was 'in a very bad condition' according to Cllr Kilner. A main wooden beam was almost cracked in two and it was advised that it should be patched with two plates. However, Elon Crowther JP, chair of Honley UDC asked if they could not help fund a new bridge. In November Cllr Ashworth, chair of South Crosland UDC highways committee, met with the Honley deputation to discuss this proposal and it was agreed to look at plans for an iron one drawn up by Holmes & Co. of Holmfirth and J. Beaumonts of Thirstin ironworks, whose other local contracts included the ironwork of the renovated Honley Wesleyan chapel. The contract was awarded to Beaumonts for £50. This iron bridge still remains - an important and unacknowledged archaeological monument to local craftsmen.[103]

ROADS

The Local Board carried out the widening of the road at Steps Fold in 1877 on land given by Joshua Beaumont & Co. By 1885 at least the Local Board was repairing the roads with dross from iron works and foundries. Lumps of this vitreous greenish-blue material can still be found where the old surface is exposed. In that year a tender was awarded to lead, ie cart, 660 tons of dross to mend roads in South Crosland including Magdale. In 1892 the Local Board bought for the purpose 400 tons of dross from Summers of Staleybridge and Leeds Steelworks. The roads were surfaced with crushed limestone giving them a bright white appearance which is evident on photos of the period.

In response to a letter from the inhabitants of Magdale in 1897, complaining that the road was 'in a most wretched state', the UDC agreed to repair it 'immediately' and in 1900, following the report of a fallen wall, Abbey & Hanson, were again instructed to see to it at once. The road was in such a bad condition by May 1901 that the trap in which Dr Smailes and his wife were riding tipped over when a wheel caught in a rut. They were shaken but uninjured. The surveyor recommended the purchase of 50 tons of unbroken and 50 tons of broken dross to repair Magdale 'Lane'. The retaining wall was repaired, the road resurfaced and two grates and 6 inch pipes put in to remove surface water in 1902. The following year the UDC agreed to replace derelict walls at Magdale. The inhabitants appear to have got both a prompt response from the council and value for their rates, more than can be said in the 21st century when it took almost two years for Kirklees council to admit responsibility for mending pot holes in the road from Steps Hill to Sandbeds![104]

One problem with a modern ring was reported in 1892. A wooden rail fence, erected by the Local Board along the Honley to Berry Brow road near Steps Mill intended 'to prevent persons walking into the river, particularly on dark nights' was vandalised. Three men from Castlehouses were prosecuted for wilful damage after Christopher Taylor, the nightwatchman for Joshua Beaumont & Co, saw the defendants pull down the whole length, some 20 yards of fencing, and break off seven posts on the river bank near the mill. He almost caught one of them who threatened to throw him in river before running off. They were fined 10s, plus 12s.6d costs each, as well as the 22s 6d damages for the fence – an expensive night out.[105]

GAS

Honley had gas lighting as early as 1859 and as we have seen, there was a gas lamp at Steps Bridge by 1863. South Crosland Local Board agreed to erect a new gas lamp at Steps Bridge in 1882 and a further three were put up on Magdale in 1889. In 1897 the UDC set lamplighters wages at Steps at 7½d. per lamp and, in 1900, it was decided that the lamp pillar at Steps Bridge would be replaced by a bracket on Steps Bridge cottages with the permission of Sir Thomas Brooke (he had been knighted the year previously). By this time there was also a domestic gas supply. T. H. Smith, a worker at the Yorkshire Penny Bank, became the first occupant in 1898 of Hillside a detached house erected during the previous winter. He could smell gas, but since the plumber failed to locate a leak he decided to try himself - by putting a lighted taper to the suspected source behind the skirting board in the front upstairs bedroom. He found a leak alright, but in the process blew up the newly furnished dining room below. Ironically, by 1901, Hillside was occupied by Henry Marsden, the manager of Honley Gas Works.[106]

In January 1914 the council requested that Honley Gas Co. reduce its charges since the four public lamps in Magdale, 'were costing the Council more and were lighted a good deal less than other lamps in the locality' which were supplied by Huddersfield Corporation. Also the residents were paying higher prices for their domestic gas. The company offered to supply and maintain each lamp at £2 each per annum if the UDC would agree to a seven year contract. This was evidently not satisfactory since in August the UDC unsuccessfully approached Huddersfield Corporation about supplying the lamps on Magdale on the same terms as the rest.[107]

PUBLIC TRANSPORT

In 1902, the tram service, which had run steam cars from Huddersfield to Berry Brow since 1892, was extended to Honley and converted to electric. Although the journey into Huddersfield took longer than the train, the tram stopped at Steps Lane end and there was no longer the need for the walk up to the railway station. In December 1904 Honley UDC wrote to the Huddersfield Tramway Committee, complaining about the state of some of the sets in the road near Steps Mill which had not been laid properly.[108]

THE POST

One facility which has certainly not improved since the 1890s is the postal service. In August 1894 it was announced that four postmen instead of three were now employed on the Honley round. In addition to the morning delivery this would allow the acceleration of deliveries and an afternoon delivery as far as Magdale![109]

Steps Mill was under the ownership of Messrs Hoyle, dyers from 1927.

WORKING LIVES – AND DEATHS

In 1891, of 78 males, around 46 worked in textile occupations and out of 88 females, 24. However, only ten men were woollen or worsted weavers compared to 13 females, showing that, in our locality at least, this trade continued to be female dominated. A decade later there was a slight reduction in weavers to nine and eleven respectively. The next most frequent male occupations in 1891 were cloth finisher and wool dyer, with seven of each. There were several changes in the textile industry at the turn of the century which affected local firms. Britain's trade was hit by increasing international competition, marked by a series of protective tariffs imposed on imports by the USA. To increase productivity new, faster Dobcross looms were installed at some mills and some firms introduced two loom working. Whereas at the time of the 1883 strike most looms operated at 50 picks a minute (a pick is a passage of the shuttle through the warp), they could now run at 90 picks or more. This meant the introduction of new pay scales and women were also increasingly being set on at lower rates than men. Dissatisfaction contributed both to a growth in trade unionism and the spread of socialist ideas. Although in only a few cases do we have details of individual Magdalers lives there is enough evidence to show that these changes affected our community.

STEPS MILL

A favoured venue for Joshua Beaumont's workers annual party in the 1890s was the Co-op Hall at Berry Brow. In 1895 a committee of ladies made the arrangements and tea was provided by Mr Taylor of Park Gate and dance music by Haigh Littlewood's band. Tom Brooke entertained with a few finely rendered songs. In January 1897 the dancing carried on until midnight and the partygoers 'wended their way home through the snow', while the following year 'humourist and mimic' master Sylvester Smith amused the gathering.

In July 1897, a ceremony was held in Steps Mill when the employees demonstrated their loyalty to the firm by assembling to present W. Dyson with a marble timepiece they had bought from the Huddersfield clock-makers Pearce & Sons to mark his marriage to Miss Beadon. The manager, Henry Mellor, gave a short speech, which is not recorded but no doubt expressed the workers' gratitude to their employers as well as best wishes to the happy couple.[110]

In August 1901, the Steps Mill treat was held at Storthes Hall, on the invitation of the head of the firm, George Pollard Armitage, whose sister, Julia Ethel, was married to Thomas James Dyson,

> The day was all that could be wished for. Waggonettes started from Honley Bridge at two o'clock, and took the route via Huddersfield and Waterloo, arriving at Kirkburton just before four o'clock. They were met on the front by Mr. Armitage, who soon had them all in the midst of enjoyments. The lads at once commenced playing cricket, the others either viewing the grounds or sitting on the lawn. However, promptly at 4-30 the bell sounded, and that, of course, brought the whole party together to have tea in front of the hall, which was well appreciated after the drive.

Music was on this occasion was provided by Kirkburton Brass Band. Henry Mellor closed the proceedings with the usual appeal for loyalty, proposing that the 'best thanks' be given to Mr. Armitage for inviting them all there that day and for the kindness and manner he had kept the whole party going. Also he hoped that the good feeling would still continue as it had done between master and men.[111]

But not everything was as harmonious as it seemed. The previous November the trade union weekly the *Yorkshire Factory Times* had reported that at Lower Steps Mill, 'the weavers, all of them women…accepted a reduction in wages proposed by the firm.' It is not clear whether this means that all the weavers were women, or only that women weavers were affected. If the former was still the case, as 30 years before, it would account for the higher proportion of female over male power loom weavers on Magdale. Either way, the women obviously didn't figure in manager Mellor's homily about 'master and men'. Even there it wasn't all good feeling. In 1902 one worker, James Holmes, was prosecuted by the firm for leaving work without giving a week's notice. He was fined 10s. 6d.[112]

In 1898, along with neighbouring Josiah's, Lower Steps Mill was visited by the Factory Inspector who ordered them to put in 'efficient fire escape appliances'. The size of the workforce is not known at this time, but just before the Great War 60 looms and 3,000 spindles were running, manufacturing meltons, beevers and other cloths.

Meanwhile, Upper Steps Mill appears to have been empty. In 1901 it was advertised 'To Let' in the *Huddersfield Examiner* as premises 'suitable for rug manufacturer or similar trade...', that is, something on a small scale - but it appears that no takers could be found to operate it.[113]

The dam was still leased by Joshua Beaumont & Co, since in July 1903 the Urban District Council wrote to them complaining about 'the offensive state' of Magdale dam after 'the water was run off and an extensive surface of decomposing mud left exposed to the rays of the sun'.

JOSIAH'S

In 1899, Josiah France & Co. was registered as a limited company with capital of £30,000 in £10 shares. The subscribers were Josiah himself, W. H. Lord, J. C. Lord, Charles Wheawill, a chartered accountant and Arthur B. Winder (Josiah's son-in-law) of Blackpool. Tom Senior, of Magdale, a fancy worsted designer was also one of the directors. Two years later, aged 30, Josiah was living at Steps Hill, next door to farmer Henry Hinchliffe. His class was given as worker, indicating that he must have still been employed as a designer, but he and his wife were wealthy enough to employ a servant, 15-year-old Beatrice Bulmer from Dodworth. Sadly, his career as director did not last long – he died in 1903.

In 1902 the firm introduced wage increases of 5% for females and 1s for males on slow looms. Some male weavers were also working 90 pick looms. Other fancy worsted manufacturers like Taylor & Lodge of Newsome had already introduced all fast looms by this time. By 1906 the mill was reported to be very busy working with overtime being worked. By then, some four box, 100 pick/minute looms had been introduced. A number of workers had been recruited to the union and several weavers' meetings were held, usually at the Railway pub at Honley Bridge, in 1908 and 1909, one addressed by local leader Allen Gee and another where pattern weavers agreed to 6d an hour.[114]

From 1899 to 1900 the 'collector' for the Honley, Brockholes and New mill district of the General Union of Weavers and Textile Workers was R. Fox of Magdale. His job was not just to collect dues but also to recruit, the *Factory Times* announcing that he 'will be glad to call on any intending member in the district'. He is not in the census the following year but may be Robert the son of Joseph Fox. Robert appears in the 1881 census as a 13-year-old unemployed woollen piecer and his father, a 66-year-old woollen weaver, was still living on Magdale in 1901 with his wife and two other adult sons.

Josiah France died aged 73 in 1905. His estate was assessed at £134,274. 9s .3d. of which his daughter, Penelope Winder, was the main beneficiary. She used some of the inheritance to build the nurses, home at Southgate, Honley, and pay a nurse's salary as a memorial to her father. It was run by Honley Nursing Association, set up in 1891 to provide nursing for the poor, with the support of Penelope's husband Dr Arthur Winder, then practising in Honley, and Josiah's sister Ann, who in 1893 donated an invalid chair.

Parkton Grove, now occupied by J. D. Crowther, was offered for sale in 1909 in an 'excellent state of repair, a considerable sum having been expended on it recently...' With electric lighting and well laid out grounds, it was described as, 'pleasantly situated in the country, but within easy reach of the town, being practically on the tram route to Honley and not far from Honley Station...'. [115]

Josiah France Ltd was listed in the 1910 *Yorkshire Trade Directory* as Fancy Worsted manufacturers, with a London Office at 21 Golden Square and Telephone No.14, Honley.[116]

DYERS

Seven men give their occupation as wool dyer in 1891. Four of these are in the same family – James Beaumont of Steps Fold and his three sons. Robert Farrar, a wool dyer, was also living on Magdale. He must be the member of the firm of that name since he is 27 and his sister Edith, who is living with him, 22, the exact ages to be the son and daughter of George W. Farrar. Another woollen dyer, Joseph Beaumont lived next door to him. By 1901 Robert was living on Jagger Lane, Honley while, ironically, George Thompson Oldham, 33, master silk dyer, was living in the Farrars' former residence at Cliff House.

In 1901, we know of only one person working at Farrar's, not from the census, but from the *Examiner* in 1950. In June that year, it reported the death of 'Honley's Oldest Resident', Joe Parkin of Mag Bridge aged 91, who had worked as mechanic at 'Magdale Dye Works' for 50 years. A Joe Parkin, 21, working as a dyer, appears on Magdale in 1881, son of weaver John Parkin. By 1901 he had become a 'Stationary Engine Tenter', possibly looking after the very engine advertised at the Magbridge dyeworks in 1892, and was back on Magdale living next door to his 82-year-old widowed mother. Perhaps he inherited his longevity from her. Joe recalled that the works was generating its own electricity before Huddersfield corporation. As well as Joe Parkin there are two other stationary engine tenters living on Magdale in 1901, Thomas Reece and Fred Bingley, as well as an engine stoker, William Bingley

Four men on Magdale were connected with silk dyeing in 1891. One was Gerald Oldham, 22, a silk dyer boarding with Mary, the widow of Joseph Bedford Donkersley who had died two years before. Whether he was a relative of the Moll Spring Oldhams I have not been able to establish. Others were Richard Sheepshank, 61, originally from Manchester and Walter Fox who lived down Early Butts (as Healdy Butts is now called), with his father, Joseph.

Woodhouse Whitworth, ten years before merely described as 'silk dyer', was promoted to 'silk dyer foreman' by 1891. He was living with his father Joseph, mother Christiana, brother George and sister Elizabeth at Steps Hill (now number 53 Magdale). Joseph, a woollen spinner, who had been one of the main organisers of the Jubilee festivities in 1887, died in 1898. George Whitworth died tragically young in March 1900. A woollen spinner, aged 31, he had been ill with heart and lung problems since the previous Christmas, and was recently spitting a lot of blood. After spending all evening in the Grove Inn he was found collapsed in the road near Steps Lane End, and wrongly assumed to be simply the worse for drink. He was carried home up Steps Hill to his mother Christiana, who although a nurse, was unable to revive him. Martha Ann Brooke of Whitegate House, a 42-year-old unwed daughter of widowed cloth finisher John Brooke, performed the laying out.

By 1901 there were three men connected with the silk dyeworks, Joe Woodhouse, 29, of Early Butts, a warehouseman, 25-year-old Fred Kinder, a silk dyer's labourer and Arnold Wright, silk dyer, the 20-year-old son of Henry Wright.

DRESSMAKERS, A SUICIDE AND STRANGE SWEEPS

In 1891, there is only one woman recorded as a dressmaker, Alice Emma Castle, the 19-year-old daughter of Firth Castle, a fancy worsted weaver who had moved from the New mill area to Magdale in the late 1870s. Alice still described herself as a dressmaker in 1901, but now was an employer working at home. Her younger sister Ann, also a dressmaker, was recorded as a worker, presumably employed by Alice. There were now three other Magdale women in this trade.

The Castle family suffered a terrible tragedy in 1903. Alice's mother, Mary Ann returned from visiting a neighbour to find her husband, Firth, hanging by a cord from the pantry ceiling, a pair of steps leant against the wall. Only 56, he had been out of work for the previous three months due to depression and had been receiving treatment under Dr Smailes. He was laid out by Leah Hobson. The family may have left Magdale two years later when Wood Cottage was again advertised for sale. Now sub-divided, it comprised a three bedroom house with an adjoining cottage. The house was occupied by Charles Dean, a 28-year-old woollen firm commercial traveller, living with his wife, infant daughter and mother in law. He may be related to the firm of Charles Dean & Sons of Reins Mill, which went bankrupt in 1900. The Castles lived in the cottage part. During renovations in the 1980s it was discovered that an area under the stairs had been walled in. It had previously been a pantry.

Another dressmaker, Gertrude Atha, 16, was recorded as working at home on her 'own account' in 1901. She was born at Armitage Bridge, where her father, Ben Lewis Atha, a keen cricketer, worked as a woolsorter at John Brooke & Sons' mill. His father, Ben, was also formerly a wool sorter and a leading member of the firm's fire brigade. In 1901, aged 36, and a foreman, Ben Lewis was living at Woodbine Cottage (55 Magdale) where his landlord was also his employer, Thomas Brooke.

On 24th August, 1907, their house was visited by two Holmfirth chimney sweeps, George and Ezra Eastwood. Ben's wife Lena was at home and agreed only to the chimney pots being swept. Since they seemed to be taking an unusually long time she went to investigate and found them on another part of the roof. They explained that they were mending slates, but she told to them to stop since that was the landlord's responsibility. On his return from work, Ben went up the ladder to find a four-foot strip of lead flashing had been taken and another cut and rolled up. The sweeps were prosecuted on the charge they 'did unlawfully and maliciously, do and commit damage, injury, or spoil, to and upon the roof of a certain dwelling-house the property of Sir Thomas Brooke, Baronet … to the amount of ten shillings'. The gist of the conversation which had taken place with Mrs Atha was reported at their trial,

'Something was said about strange sweeps, and the defendants said they were not strange, and they and their father had been carrying on the business for about forty years. She

told them that she was very sorry that she had got them into trouble, but that if they were innocent they had nothing to fear... ',

Although the prosecution conceded that the evidence was entirely circumstantial, both defendants were fined 5s, with 12s costs and 5s damages. A solicitor, Mr. Charles H. Marshall, wrote to the papers complaining that they had not had a fair hearing. He believed them to be trustworthy since they had swept his chimneys for years.

RAILWAYS

A few railway related occupations are recorded. In 1881 Arthur son of John Brooke of Whitegate House was employed as a railway pointsman, but in 1891, he was shown as a cloth finisher, like his father. In 1901 he was again recorded as a pointsman.

In 1891 there was a 'retired railway foreman', Rowland Sykes Haigh, a widower of 63. He was one of the Haighs whom we met in 1848, now returned to Throstlenest under very different circumstances - boarding with George and Ann Brooke (the author's great-great-grandparents) and their eight children, aged seven to 21. Was this uncomfortable arrangement by choice and what had happened to his own relatives ? The last one known on Magdale was his brother Rockley, recorded in 1881 as a labourer, unemployed who, although described as married was living alone, next-door-but-one to the Brookes.

Edwin Drake was recorded as store keeper and railway labourer. A widower, he lived at Magbridge with his sister, (the head of household), brother, son and daughter. Not long after the 1901 census his son, Jim, a 23-year-old cloth finisher, who had suffered from consumption for 15 years, was found one evening in Church Street, Honley, bleeding from the mouth. He died soon after, the second Magdaler within little over a year taken by this disease.[117]

LIVING ON MEANS

A new category appeared in the census for 1891, that of 'living on means', retired people with an income from savings or capital. These include Ann Roberts, 60, who lived alone, Benjamin Crowther, 69, who was living with his sister Mary, (the widow of Joseph Bedford Donkersley), and Sarah Dearnley, a widow, living at Steps, aged 59. This could be a precarious existence. In April of that year Sarah Dearnley advertised the sale of her furniture in the *Examiner*, with the explanation she was 'declining housekeeping'. This echoes the term used in adverts for mill machinery, when the vendor is described as declining business. Often this could indicate a bankruptcy and this may be the case here since, in July, Thomas W. Dearnley of Victoria mill, Honley, stated in the bankruptcy court that he had sold furniture and machinery in order to try and clear his debts. If this Sarah is the widow of the late Thomas Dearnley of Townhead, Honley, woollen manufacturer, then Thomas W. was her son and his business difficulties could account for her plight.

FARMING

James Jessop was still at Steps in 1891, a farmer, aged 69, now living alone. He died in 1900. In 1901 there is only one farmer, Henry Hinchliffe, 35, the tenant of Steps Farm. It is recollected that his horse returned home of its own accord when it tired of waiting outside the pub he visited at the end of his milk round. The author's grandfather, George Brooke, as a boy, used to help Henry's wife Sarah un-harness it and put the cart away. Sarah seems to have been the driving force behind the business, since following her

George Brooke of Magdale, holding the slate in a 1907 photograph
of Miss Evans' infant class at Honley National School.
Inset, George in Throstlenest garden, aged five.

John W. Tunstall, sitting at the right hand side of the boys' class of 1894 of Honley
National School. A young head teacher, George Borwell, is seated in the centre.

death in 1915 Henry gave up the farm and moved into Honley. He tried unsuccessfully to claim a tenant right payment from Thomas Brooke, Healey House, for improvements, but the landlord's agent told the court that repairs to walls, fences and windows had not been carried out. Alfred Beever, a former coal miner, took over the tenancy.[118]

The only other agricultural occupation recorded in 1901 is John Kinder, 34, 'carter on farm'. A related occupation is that of Henry Wright, aged 50, (possibly the naturalist friend of James Jessop), who is recorded as a self employed market gardener, working at home.

TEACHERS

The expansion of state education following the 1870 Education Act was reflected in the increase in the number of teachers living on Magdale. As early as 1861 there had been a 'Schoolmistress' living at Steps, Matilda, the 53-year-old sister of manufacturer, David Platt. In 1881, Ada (19), the daughter of Robert Booth, the book-keeper at Steps Mill, is described as an Assistant School Teacher and by 1891 she has been promoted to School Teacher. Edith, 20, the daughter of John Brooke of Whitegate House is also a School Teacher at this time, while a married man, Fred Green, 26, appears with the differing title of Assistant Schoolmaster. A decade later, there are two Elementary schoolteachers Florence Ann Booth, 20, single, living with her widowed mother next door to the Athas and Ernest Bendelow, aged 24, living with his in-laws. He had married Sarah, a former millworker, the daughter of the late James Lancaster, farmer. His sister who lived with them is a tailoress.

In 1881 Isabella, the 16-year-old daughter of Mary and Joseph Bedford Donkersley, appears as a Teacher of Music. She was a talented violinist and in 1883 performed at a concert given by Mr Haddock's School of Music at Bradford Church Institute. The piece she chose, according to the critic, 'scarcely affording the exact opportunity she requires for showing off her ability. Her instrument, moreover, can hardly be called a good one for solo purposes'. The Miss Donkersley of Honley who played the piano may be her sister Martha Lucy. Between 1884 and 1890 Isabella, or 'Bell' as she was called there, attended the Royal College of Music. There were whispers of scandal since her tutor, Henry Holmes, gave her extra lessons alone in his rooms where he was known to lecture his female students on atheism and socialism and other topics unsuitable for young ladies. On leaving the RCM she continued to live in London, but kept close contact with both her sister and now widowed mother at Ivy Cottage. She earned a number of rave reviews for some of her performances including the premier of works by new composers, which she now played on a valuable Guadanigni violin loaned to her for life by a rich patron.

Through her love of music she met August Jaeger, a manager at Novello's music publishing firm and a leading critic. His family, while not exactly refugees, had fled the repressive cultural and political atmosphere of Bismark's Germany and arrived in London from Dusseldorf in 1878. August was a close friend and collaborator of Edward Elgar to whom he introduced Isabella. Elgar found her 'charming' and 'my wife is also charmed with her'. The Jaegers regularly corresponded with the Elgars and occasionally visited them. August was portrayed in Elgar's 'Enigma Variations' as Nimrod – the mighty 'hunter', the English for Jaeger. In real life though, August was a frail looking man with small spectacles and a large moustache. In 1898 he married Isabella in Kensington where Isabella's sister Martha Lucy and her new husband John William Tunstall acted a witnesses. Isabella and August honeymooned in Dusseldorf and, due to her husbands' nationality, she became a German citizen.

Isabella still came to stay with sister Lucy on Magdale, sometimes accompanied by August, who 'spent a few quiet & happy days' here in 1899. His references to 'my wife's home in Yorkshire', shows that the couple felt she still had roots here. The following year Isabella gave birth to a daughter and in 1901 to a son. A photo in August's biography depicts them at Ivy Cottage with the youngest still a babe-in-arms. Isabella had also apparently kept her local dialect, since the children were referred to as 'the bairns'.

Their happiness was to be short-lived. At the end of 1904, August became ill with the first signs of TB. Over the following years his health steadily declined, despite stays in the health resort of Davos in Switzerland, from where he wrote postcards to the Tunstalls. Isabella had again to take up music teaching to help their flagging finances. He died in 1909. Isabella continued to live in London but she and the children maintained their friendship with the Magdale relatives.[119]

Mother Mary Donkersley died in 1899 and Martha Lucy had continued to live in the family home at Ivy Cottage after her marriage. Her husband, John William Tunstall, was described in 1901 as an Assistant Elementary School Teacher, aged 36, originally from Little Broughton in Cumberland. They had a three-month-old son, Joseph William Brian. John W. Tunstall was to serve as a teacher at Honley C of E school for 46 years. He was a man of many interests and deeply held beliefs. He shared an interest in music with both Lucy and Isabella and was choirmaster at Honley Church for 26 years. In his younger days he was involved in organising cricket and football teams. He later acted as treasurer for Honley & District Nursing Association, which took over the running of the Southgate nurses' home built in memory of Josiah France.

Sometimes he felt compelled to express his strongly held opinions in letters to the *Huddersfield Examiner* which could be quite pompous and school-masterish in tone. In September 1898 he responded to John T. Haigh, who, in a letter headed Priestcraft, accused the vicar of Honley of refusing to officiate at the burial of a non-believer in the cemetery. JW defended the vicar's stance, claiming, 'Everybody must admit that it is downright mockery to read the Church burial services over the body of anyone who, when he was alive, thought the whole thing a farce'. Those who object should conduct their own service. Haigh replied by saying that the Vicar, after consulting the Bishop of Wakefield, had admitted he was wrong and had apologised. The correspondence grew increasingly irate and the editor had to cut out an offensive passage from one of Tunstall's epistles. J.W. remained adamant that it was the Vicar who had been wronged,

> If certain men with a supposed grievance would meet their clergy half way in the spirit
> of Christian charity, instead of standing aloof and misconstruing their every action, we
> should soon have very few ministers trying to drive their engines with cold water, and a less
> number of men trying to drive theirs without the fuel necessary for holy and peaceful lives.

The war of words raged for a month until the editor announced 'This correspondence must now cease'. [120]

There is no doubt, however, that his strict moral sense was founded on genuine compassion and an abhorrence of injustice and violence, not only against people but also other creatures. He expressed approval for the St George's Club for Children since, 'Its members promise, among other things, to befriend where possible, those who are in need – the weak, the poor and the aged; not to torture any dumb animal, not to rob a bird's nest, not to wantonly destroy wild flowers', He also supported the Guild of St George, founded by John Ruskin in 1871, which he described as:

> a great organised attempt to roll back the torrent of pauperism in Great Britain, to raise
> a new generation of labourers, and to manufacture happiness, not by state machinery, but
> by individual effort. Its members bound themselves that they would not deceive or cause

to be deceived, nor hurt nor cause to be hurt, nor rob, nor cause to be robbed any human being for their gain or pleasure but would strive to save and comfort all gentle life, and guard and perfect all natural beauty upon earth. It is a great scheme of true Socialism, wherein the individual must be true to himself, so that he cannot be false to any man.[121]

SOCIALISTS

John Tunstall was perhaps more literary than most but he was not the only Magdaler with a social conscience. While he held to a Christian, Ruskinite, 'Tory-Socialism', other socialist beliefs was reviving with a religious fervour of their own, reflected in the expansion of trade unionism and the rise of the parliamentary Labour Party.

Honley Labour, later Socialist, Club was affiliated to the Independent Labour Party founded in 1893, but was more militant than the national leadership. There were several members at various times on Magdale, the most consistent being Hamlet Brooke. He had joined Honley Labour Club as it then was by 1895, aged 19, when the first membership book was opened and remained a member until during the Great War. Hamlet worked for 50 years, his entire life, at Josiah France's rising to become a pattern weaver until his death aged 64. In 1901 he was living at Throstlenest with his widowed mother Anne, three sisters, of whom one was a worsted weaver and two were woollen weavers, and three brothers - Mark, a worsted piece presser, Havelock a cloth tenter and Norman, aged 17, assistant to a worsted spinner. All the brothers joined the Labour/Socialist club at some time or another, Mark for only about a year.[122]

The club's fortunes fluctuated with the political climate. Between 1901 and 1905 it practically collapsed, but grew rapidly with the wave of enthusiasm which carried the Socialist MP Victor Grayson to victory in 1907. Charles Henry Boothroyd, a scribbling engineer of Magbridge and his sons Joe and Willie aged 18 and 16, joined together in 1906. However they all resigned after the election. When the Socialist club acquired new premises at Jagger Lane in 1911 one of the trustees was Edwin Charlesworth of Magbridge, a twister-in. Several other names in the membership book could be those of Magdalers, but they are too commonplace to be sure.

THE FIRST WORLD WAR

The Great War brought Magdale suddenly and violently into the arena of international politics. At least one person was expecting it. J W Tunstall's brother-in-law had warned him of the threat of German militarism and that 'Der Tag' – 'the Day' - when war would come was inevitable. In April 1917, amid the slaughter, Tunstall called upon people to mark St George's day, describing the significance of the saint... 'history and its ancient attendant, mythology, supply us with a figure whose name and symbol take a foremost place in thousands of branches of the many societies organised purposely for the creation of human happiness, the inculcation of patriotism and the amelioration of suffering'. As a patriotic symbol the saint was embodied in the St George's Society, 'for the cementing into one common brotherhood of affection all Englishmen wherever they may be scattered...' but he warned people to distinguish between 'flag flying' and 'flag flaunting'. He must have been acutely aware of the dangers of unbridled nationalism since, due to the pressure of anti-German feeling at the outbreak of war his widowed sister-in-law Isabella had felt compelled to anglicise her name from Jaeger to Hunter.

Most people were swept along by events. Among the first to enlist on 5th September, 1914 were young Archie Munro and his elder brother William, sons of Daniel Munro of Steps Cottage, both workers at Josiah France's, who joined the Duke of Wellington's

Regiment of Kitchener's army. They were sent to France the following year. William, aged 27, was reported missing in action on 29th July, 1916 and 19-year-old Archie was killed on the 12th October. He was awarded the Military Medal. It was not until April 1917 that Daniel Munro received confirmation that William was dead.[123]

Henry Parkin, born in 1892, (the son of Joe, engineer at Magbridge dyeworks), a former scholar at Honley Church School and member of the Conservative Club who worked at Eastwood Bros' Thirstin Mill, joined in November 1915. A gunner in the Royal Field Artillery, he was awarded a first class certificate in signalling and telegraphy and was sent to the front the following June. He was killed on the 15th October, 1916. According to his officer Lieutenant J.C Thompson who wrote a condolence letter to his parents, he was seriously wounded from shell fire and died minutes later on his way to the dressing station, 'Gunner Parkin was one of the best signallers in the battery and always did his duty cheerfully and well...' His brother Albert, a finisher at Crowther's in Milnsbridge, also joined up as a RFA gunner in March 1916. He was killed in May 1918, 'the 'only surviving son of Mr and Mrs Joe Parkin'.[124]

George Earnshaw, aged 19, a worker at Thirstin Mill serving with the Scottish Rifles, was shot by sniper on 14th April, 1917, 'another member of William Brooke's bible class to make the supreme sacrifice...' commented the *Examiner*. This became a double tragedy. A month later, when Jane Beever of Steps Farm was delivering the milk, she found his father, Samuel Earnshaw, a widower, aged 57, hanging from the ceiling. He was cut down and neighbour J. W. Tunstall tried artificial respiration until Dr Smailes arrived to pronounce him dead. His daughter Jane, who had been running the household since the death of her mother, told the inquest that he had been suffering from asthma and bronchitis but nothing was mentioned, in the newspaper account at least, about his recent loss.[125]

Another family had better news. On 11th August, 1917, John William Hobson received a letter from his son Fred who had been missing since 5th May to say he was a prisoner in Germany. Fred survived the war but never fully recovered, suffering from a recurrence of 'trench foot' throughout his life.[126]

However, not everyone agreed with the war, which, for religious or political reasons, or both, they considered futile and barbaric. The Huddersfield area provided some of the strongest opposition to the war. Even among socialists the response to war was divided. Mark Brooke became one of many local conscientious objectors and after a spell in Wormwood Scrubs was sent to work in an oil shale quarry at Uphall in West Lothian. His brother Hamlet however, a member of the Socialist Club, joined the Royal Artillery. Other objectors from Honley ended up in Dartmoor gaol. Not long after the armistice Honley Socialist Club invited John Maclean, the Glasgow Socialist, on a speaking tour of the area from 26th May to 1st June, 1919. A supporter of the Russian revolution, he had been gaoled in Peterhead prison for his opposition to the war. At least one Magdaler, George Brooke, was among the crowd at Honley Market Place, since he recollected that his boss found out he was there and warned him against mixing with 'folk like that'.[127]

A SHORT SEQUEL

It may be a cliché to say that a different world emerged after the Great War, but there is no doubt that it had a dramatic impact on the lives of those who participated or who lost love ones. It also accelerated many social and technological trends only barely apparent before 1914. This period therefore is an appropriate close for a chapter in the story of Magdale. With the 1920s, we also move into the realm where memory and oral tradition supplement documentary evidence. However pre-war Magdale lived on so long as the individuals and institutions of that era survived.

Joshua Beaumont & Co occupied Steps Mill until 1927 when there was a fire, although whether this helped put them out of business is not recorded. Later that year the mill was occupied by Messers Hoyle, dyers, who installed a new boiler, having being warned by the council that they were liable for any damage done to Steps Bridge in the process. It continued as a dyeworks until a fire in 1982 severed its links with the textile industry.[128]

The four-storey part of Upper Steps Mill was demolished prior to the First World War, and extant photos show the waterwheel exposed in the process. Whether this was before or after its acquisition by Josiah France is not clear. Only the two story building was retained. This was later used as a canteen for the mill workers – the building and road alongside it are still referred to as 'the canteen' by locals. Josiah's also took over the dam and the associated allotments. Josiah's later became a subsidiary of Huddersfield Fine Worsteds which stopped production in 1975. Queens Square Mill and Magdale dam were then taken over by Bradford firm of Illingworth Morris and sold off (some would say asset stripped) ending their association with the textile industry in the Honley area.

Although agricultural activity continued, it ceased to be the main source of livelihood for any of the residents. After the Second World War when it was sold off by the Brooke estate, Steps Farm was stripped of its land on Netherton Moor leaving only two small adjacent fields. However Magdale does have a small place in the history of agriculture. In the mid 30's Harry Ferguson, then living at Dungarth House in Southgate, Honley, carried out trials of his new plough three-point linkage system in the large flat field at Early Butts, between the goit and the river bend. The tractor was driven by Magdale man Billy Quantrill. After partnerships with David Brown in 1936 and later Henry Ford in the USA, Ferguson struck out on his own and the *Examiner* commented in 1949, '…the man who watched his new tractors ploughing a field at Magdale twenty years ago may be richer by about £80m.'. Although it was in fact only the plough link that was new at this time Magdale certainly played a part in the rise of 'the Tractor King'.[129]

Sir Thomas Brooke, who died in 1909, left his property at Steps and Magdale to his nephew and namesake who lived at Healey House. Most of the houses were sold off in the 1920s and the track which ran from Steps Hill to Sandbeds was donated to South Crosland UDC becoming a public highway. A strip of land was also provided to extend the road directly to Steps Bridge past the rear of Steps Farm, but the record of the transfer was lost when this part of South Crosland merged with Holmfirth UDC in 1939 and the land was subsequently built on.

Several families continued to have a long association with Magdale. J. W. Tunstall remained active in the church and the community propagating his strong moral views. In 1920 he wrote 'a very nice letter' to S. L. Mosley, by then curator of the Tolson Memorial Museum, explaining, 'There is so much I admire and enjoy in your articles

Billy Quantrill (far left) with Harry Ferguson and team testing the revolutionary three point linkage system. (Photo - Thanks to Neil Littlewood, Billy Quantrill's great-grandson)

Magdalers in the early 20th century. Possibly all Brookes, but only brothers Hamlet (*back row left*), Mark (back centre), Havelock (*back second from right*) and Norman (*sitting nursing a plant*) have been identified. (From the Boocock Collection)

in the *Huddersfield Examiner* (Nature Around Huddersfield) that I can scarcely find the heart to draw your attention to what I will call "the fly in the ointment"... It is difficult for me to understand why it is necessary to kill only for show purposes'. Seth explained that, although some killing was necessary for scientific research, he agreed about collecting unnecessary specimens or using butterflies or feathers for decoration. Both Seth and Mr Tunstall shared the belief that Christians should have a reverence for all forms of life.[130]

When his wife Lucy died in 1922. Isabella's sister-in-law, Joanna Jaeger, known as 'Donnie' came to help him housekeep at Ivy Cottage. In 1938 he was pictured in the *Examiner* in the pretty rock garden he had constructed at the cottage. His son Brian was also multi-talented with interests as wide as art, railways and travel and accomplishments ranging from music to mountaineering. He worked as a graphic artist and was also skilled in watercolours, which appeared in Huddersfield Art Society exhibitions. (A picture of Langdale Pikes, is in the author's possession). In March 1948 he addressed the Society on 'the ever-growing trend of thoughtless planning in the town and countryside', asserting that 'artistic and aesthetic amenities should he preserved wherever possible' and that more public interest was needed to avert such 'spoliation'. Some of his sketches of local scenes signed 'JWBT' were used as vignettes at the head of the column by Puck in the *Huddersfield Examiner* in the 1940s and 50s and his recollections about the family connection with Jaeger and Elgar were published in the paper in 1966.[131]

Ben Lewis Atha followed in the footsteps of his father Ben Atha senior, who had been one of the first members of the South Crosland Local Board, by being elected to the UDC in 1917. When he retired from work in 1932 he had been employed by the Brookes of Armitage Bridge for 58 years. He died aged 72 in 1937. His 39-year-old son Reginald continued to work for the same firm.

The tradition of working men naturalists continued on Magdale. Norman Brooke, who appears in an early 1900's group photograph of the male Brookes, characteristically holding a plant specimen, joined the Yorkshire Naturalists Union in 1925 and a number of other Magdalers, including his brothers were involved in Honley Naturalist Society. Norman became a renowned medical herbalist, with a consulting room in a hut near his house at Hillcrest. Hamlet Brooke of Throstlenest was a member of Honley Naturalist Society for 35 years until his sudden death on 9th December, 1939, when he was found by a policeman at Newtown garage having apparently died from a heart attack on the way home. At his inquest his brother Havelock said Hamlet had never been attended by a doctor in his life. He was described as 'a well known naturalist and lecturer' throughout the Huddersfield area and his obituary simply refers to him as a 'naturalist'.

The author's father recollects how Hamlet led a nature study class from Honley school on a ramble and could name almost every botanical specimen collected, including the Latin terms. Sundays would be spent on long rambles into the surrounding countryside with his metal collecting case. He was an associate of naturalist Joe Allsop of Gatehead, known as 'Th'owd Scout', (a close friend of S. L. Mosley), who visited Magdale with a greengrocer's cart pulled by a donkey. An occupation that also earned him the nickname 'ready-money Joe'.[132]

As we have seen, Joe Parkin, the engineer at Farrars' dyeworks who lost both his sons in the Great War, lived until 1950. When he died aged 91 in Deanhouse Hospital (formerly the workhouse) he was Honley's oldest resident. He reminisced how he shook hands with Buffalo Bill at the Earl's Court exhibition in 1887 and, as a boy, had watched cock-fighting, commenting 'there weren't so many policemen then', but he saw no attraction in modern spectator sports like football, or as he put it, sitting 'half-starved' [frozen],

Brooke women outside Throstlenest, Ada Nestor, nee Brooke, standing in the door way and (*seated from left*), Annie Brooke, (Tanny), Anne Brooke nee Greenwood, Ellen Moss nee Brooke (Telly) holding her son Joe Willy and Emma Woodhouse nee Brooke holding her son Norman.

(From the Boocock Collection)

Honley Naturalists outing to Askern, near Doncaster.

watching 'lads kick a ball through a couple of sticks'. Renowned as a local historian, a wealth of local knowledge died with him.[133]

We began this book with a quotation from a better known local historian, Mary Jagger, who wished to record the way of life before, '... the old is changed into the new.' That pace of change has accelerated far more quickly than she could ever have envisaged. While Magdale is still picturesque and retains a lot of its original character despite the encroachments of suburbia and commercial activity, the mills around which the settlement grew are now divorced from manufacturing and accommodate various service industries employing only a fraction of the hundreds once employed in textiles. Along with the textile industry a whole culture, language and way of life has disappeared. In many ways life in Magdale in the 1960s bore more resemblance to the 1860s than it does to life today, so rapid and profound have been recent changes in society and social attitudes.

It is up to the reader to decide whether those changes have been for the better or not. In 1950 the *Examiner* carried a picture of 'A Peaceful dale near Honley' captioned, 'Magdale, near Honley, has always a quiet charm, which is undisturbed by the thunder of the traffic of commerce along the main Woodhead Road at the foot of the little valley.' Sadly this is no longer the case. If Magdale has retained some charm, it certainly is no longer quiet. It is symptomatic of the frenetic technology-driven lifestyle that has forced the demise of a way of life which, though harder and poorer in material goods, was certainly richer in humanity.

Four of Brian Tunstall's sketches of Magdale scenes.

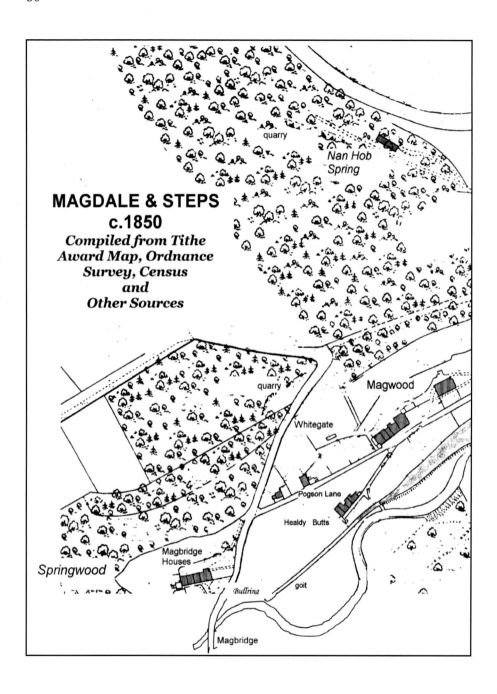

MAGDALE & STEPS
c.1850
Compiled from Tithe
Award Map, Ordnance
Survey, Census
and
Other Sources

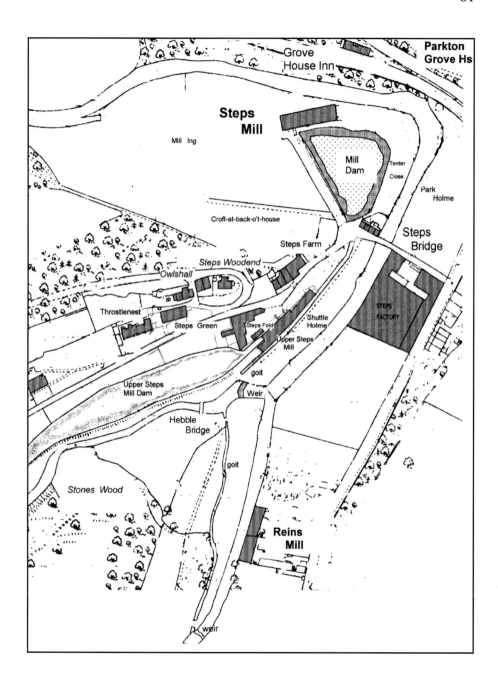

APPENDIX
Literary references to Magdale from the local press
MAG-DALE

I've gloomed in the city, that desert of men,
While thirsting for woodland, green, meadow and glen,
But now on an oasis whose waters ne'er fail,
I glow 'midst they sweetness, O lovely Mag-dale.

Oft, childlike, my vision I close to the day,
And dream till I think that I'm far, far away,
And then in a moment of blissful surprise,
On thee, my loved valley, how banquet mine eyes.

But 'tis not thy beauty alone doth impart,
The rapturous feeling that whirls in my heart,
'Tis mixed with emotions life cannot destroy,
That gush from the source of youth, infant, and boy.

This spot whence my cottage now smiles upon thee,
Was once the fair seat of thy famed 'cademy,
Where frequent a rival, and ever a friend,
I met with its worthies in lore to contend.

Mag river, that babbles or brawls at my feet-
When its features were brighter its breath was more sweet-
In summer and boyhood, I playfully pressed,
As blithe as a sunbeam, or trout in its breast.

Yon hallowed Stoneswood, which I daily regard,
I've trod as a truant, a lover, a bard;
And had I the power I would quickly restore,
Its shade spreading branches to wave as of yore.

Thy stories of marvellous agencies still,
I hear with delight and mystical thrill,
For though science may scout the hour was divine,
When the spring of Nan-hob and her neighbours ran wine.

Thy witches are gone, but the fairy-folks good,
Yet frolic 'tis said, in the Nook of Springwood,
And dance to the fountain-fall's moon mellowed glee,
Around the charmed trunk of the twin beechen tree.

I've gloomed in the city, that desert of men,
While thirsting for woodland, green, meadow and glen,
But now on an o'sis whose waters ne'er fail,
I glow' midst they sweetness, O lovely Mag-dale.

Huddersfield Chronicle 7th December, 1876

THE LILY OF MAG VALLEY

'Ah, let me drink sweet maid', said I,
As in the margin of Spring Wood,
The moss illumined fountain nigh,
The Lily of Mag Valley stood,
Watching the pearl drops as they gushed,
From the rock casket cool and bright,
And down amongst the flowerets rushed,
Chanting the praise of freedoms light.

It was an hour of gladsome beam,
When every bush sent forth its mirth,
While bluebells thronging there made seem,
As if the heavens had come to earth.
And as I looked upon the maid,
Who bore her cup with Hebe's grace,
I marvelling bowed and gently said,
'This surely's a celestial place'.

To drain the precious draft I burned,
Which she presented pale and meek,
But when the goblet I returned,
The pink rose huddled on her cheek,
And like a fawn off bounded she,
As soon as my parched lips were blest,
And left a deeper thirst to be,
A quenchless fire within my heart.

Huddersfield Examiner 27th May, 1882

MAGDALE IN MAY - An Old Man's Reverie

O Mag, how fair thy winding stream,
Thy hanging woods and meadows bonnie,
Thy lonely nooks with babbling brooks,
Thy breezy crags so wild and sunny.
Thy woods are deckt with bluebells sweet,
With bracken green and waving heather,
And for a carpet for our feet,
Brown leaves and grasses knit together.

An old man seeks thy birken shade,
To spend an hour or two in thinking;
A man who outlived his trade,
Who used to keep the handloom clinking.
His loom is silent now and still,
His bobbins done, his shuttles rotting,
They've put him on the pension list,
He's living now on what he's getting.

continues....

Sing on, thou bonnie speckled thrush,
Thy song so mellow, blithe and cheery;
I like to hear thy gurgling gush-
A song so sweet can never weary.
I'll hie me to yon dizzy crag,
That frowns above thy winding river,
And ther'll I sing your praises Mag,
While thou roll'st bubbling on for ever.

Flow still, sweet Mag, among thy braes,
Thy meadows green, and moorland heather,
Thy scenery charms my aged gaze,
Thour't grand in every kind of weather,
Now bluebells scent thy birkenshaws,
The primrose on your banks is springing,
And just to break thy calm repose,
The wild birds are thy praises singing.

J. P. Hoyle of Honley, *The Worker,* May 1911

COUNTRY RAMBLES – HONLEY

I indolently sauntered from Honley, entered Magdale and forthwith went to Nan Hob well where I knew that lavish nature would not begrudge me to drink of the coolest crystal that ever slaked man or animal. I say animal because I had barely done drinking before I saw a young frog calmly eyeing me and evidently gratified that I was not afraid of partaking in his native element...I, of course, gave over drinking, and then turned my attention to this beautiful and harmless creature...Nan Hob Well is uniquely situated. Its retreat is most picturesque, and its sylvan shades are very charming. I knew that on this occasion, the burning sun was flaming overhead, but so protected was this grotto, by the open leaves of the oak, the ash and the horse chestnut and the sycamore, that his piercing rays could not pierce it. Here the 'fern's green fronds enwrapped the rocks', and 'mosses green revealed their nests,' while, 'charming songsters filled the air', and 'frisking lambs the woodlands roved'. There were thousands of living creatures which courted my attention, but my pretty frog surpassed them all. Fixed in the crevice of the crystal fountain he seemed the coolest and most platonic creature I had ever seen...At this moment I was disturbed in my observations by the approach of a band of irreverent School Board educated youths who would have made short work of froggy had I not hid him in a crevice out of their reach. In the meantime, two or three neatly-clad damsels approached, filled their cans with water and hastened away just as a band of ruffians came up, and with oaths, betting language and indecent gestures turned what was a moment before, a peaceful and solitary retreat, into a pandemonium where nought but man was vile. As I left I felt I should have been delighted to have seen the backs of these men laid bare and the cat used mercilessly on them.

The Huddersfield Echo 9th July, 1887

NOTES AND REFERENCES

1. *Coin Finds of the Huddersfield District* , Graham Teasdill, Edited By E. W. Aubrook, Tolson Memorial Museum; *History of Honley* Mary Jagger, Ch. xvi (Honley 1914). For a more recent examination of the coins see Chris Rudd, *Coin News* January 2017 pp.39-40.
2. Redmond, Dr George ' The mystery of Magdale' *Huddersfield Examiner* 17ᵗʰ August, 1996.
3. Place names of West Yorkshire.
4. 'The Country around Holmfirth and Glossop', Geological Survey of Britain, 1933 p.73.
5. The Almondbury parish register, on microfilm, Huddersfield Local History Library (HLHL). Some of the entries, particularly for the early eighteenth century are practically illegible, so there may be some omissions or errors of transcription in the following account.
6. For early fulling mills and the Roberts see Crump & Ghorbal, *History of the Huddersfield Woollen Industry.* Tolson Museum Publications (1935)
7. The South Crosland township overseer of the poor account book, in West Yorkshire Archive Service, Kirklees. Also for Ann Dyson, see account by Philip Ahier, HLHL.
8. A Paul Brook lived at Magbridge in 1773 perhaps indicating that he and John Brook, father of the lame Paul, were related.
9. I am very grateful to David Boocock for this and other information about the Oldfields. He comments, "When James' wife baptised her child in 1787 (18 days before husband James was buried) she was anxious to have herself declared a widow. There was a threepence stamp tax introduced in October of 1783 for every parish Registry entry. I suspect that she was exempt if widowed."
10. *Leeds Mercury* (LM) 28ᵗʰ February & 7ᵗʰ November, 1801
11. Register of Deeds (D.E) I.281:395 1790 - RD.DC:135.577. John Carter joiner, Mag Bridge, house at Thirstin/Bottoms, formerly dyehouse. Thirstin Mill, Honley. DT Jenkins, *The West Riding Wool Textile Industry 1770-1835*; Land Tax Returns (LTR) - John Carter for 'scribbling mill' (first reference to one in Honley. c.f. Factory Commissioners Report). Removal of a garden from a house at the bottom of Thirstin Road has revealed an arch, which is probably the remains of the water wheel race.
12. Dartmouth Estate Terrier, Estate Office. Thanks to the agents of the estate for allowing me access to these documents, now in Leeds Archives. The photocopy of the page bearing the plan of Upper Steps Mill and the rental for Steps and Magdale was given to me by the late Mr John Naylor of Magdale. I have not seen the original. '1805 terrier' is hand written on it. David Boocock believes this is incorrect and that it dates from the 1820s, since the names do not fit in with the genealogical research.
13. The Enclosure Award and Map is in HLHL.
14. *Huddersfield Examiner* (HE), *Huddersfield Chronicle* (HC) 17ᵗʰ November,1866; HE 8ᵗʰ February, 1868.
15. *Leeds Mercury* May 1795.
16. DT Jenkins op. cit. p.306
17. WYAS, Kirklees - (KC 165:124) For background to Inghams see *Yorkshire Archaeological Journal* Vol. 55 (1983) Nussey, John 'Blake Hall in Mirfield…'
18. LM 9ᵗʰ March, 1805
19. Jagger, op. cit. ; HE 3ʳᵈ June,1893, report on reopening of Wesleyan Chapel.
20. Annals of Yorkshire p206; thanks to Michael Day for the *Leeds Intelligencer* reference. Additional material on Steps Mill, particularly the rebuilding after the fire, can be found in his book *Wool and Worsit – a history of textiles in the Holme Valley* , Huddersfield 2013 pp.330-336.
21. Alan Brooke & Lesley Kipling, *Liberty or Death*, (Huddersfield Local History Society 2012)
22. *Leeds Intelligencer* (LI) 20ᵗʰ September, 1819, John Nowell note books West Yorkshire Archive Service, Huddersfield Local Studies Library, KC312 13/16; *Baines History, Directory and Gazeteer* 1823.
23. LM 19ᵗʰ December, & 26ᵗʰ December, 1829. See also letters from J Whitacre and Joseph Bradley on same controversy. LM 16ᵗʰ October, 1830
24. LM 21ˢᵗ June,1828. A vivid account of the anxiety caused by the fear of rabies following a dog bite can be found in Charlotte Bronte's *Shirley* where the eponymous heroine cauterises her own wound, an incident said to be based on the real life experience of Emily Bronte.
25. LM 26ᵗʰ October, 1833.
26.The painting is now in the possession of a Magdale resident from whom framed canvas copies are available.
27. LM 3ʳᵈ March, 1827. The Land Tax Returns (LTR) for mill 1829-30 refers to 'Beaumont, William, or occupiers'.
28. *Halifax & Hudderfield Express* 16ᵗʰ June, 1832.
29. *Voice of the West Riding* 7ᵗʰ September, 1833; *Halifax Guardian* 29ᵗʰ February, 1840.
30. *Northern Star* (NS) 16ᵗʰ June, 1839; 20ᵗʰ June, 1840, 30ᵗʰ October, 1841.

31. *Leeds Times* (LT) 21st January, NS 21st January, 1843, LM 4th February, 1843.

32. Detail provided by the censuses and ordnance survey maps enable us from now on to build up a more accurate picture of the population and the physical environment they inhabit. The survival of the Tithe Map from 1847 even allows us to locate some people in specific dwellings.

33. HC 18th May, 1850; 8th January, 7th May, 1853.

34. LM 17th February, 1849

35. HC 9th November, 1850

36. HC 14th June,1851

37. Jagger, op.cit. p.308; 1908 HEW 18 Jul: Sir Thomas Brooke, Bart, obituary. It records: born 1830, son of Thomas Brooke, Honley, educated at Cheltenham College, 1847 joined firm. Lived 1854-58 at Fenay Lodge, moved to Northgate House (later residence of William Brooke) and then to Armitage Bridge House. In 1859, founder of Volunteers, supporter of Mechanics Institute and Technical School. Founder of Antiquarian Society which became Yorks Archaeological and Topographical Society of which he was president. Described as Liberal, tolerant and art lover. First marriage to Eliza Vickerman on day of battle of Alma, she died less than a year later in childbirth. Only son Francis Thomas Brooke died 1872. 1860 married Ms A Dewar, died 1901 than 1902 married widow of Rev. Forster, daughter of Thomas Priestly of Taylor Hill (c.43).

38. Letter from Joseph Gledhill, Steps Mill, to Walter Gledhill, Richland Co.,Ohio, 29th August, 1847. Thanks to Roger Bird of Oakland, California and his cousin Lloyd Gledhill for background information on Joseph and permission to quote from a transcript and copy of the letter.

39. LM 5th February, 1850

40. Haigh Letters, Yorkshire Archaeological Society. I am very grateful to Jennifer Stead for providing me with transcripts of this source. LM 1st April, 15th April,1848

41. *History of Honley* (pp.336-337)

42. HE 13th January, 1855; HE 16th December, 1854;

43. HE 25th January, 1868. It was probably the glass panes of this weaving shed which were riddled by hailstones in a storm in 1859, HE 23rd July, 1859.

44. HE 12th October 1861. Joshua and Magdalen Beaumont survived a train crash at Staleybridge (sic) in 1863 (HE 22nd August). For a time they lay at Parkton Grove in 'a precarious state'.

45. HEW 22nd June, 1872; 10th April, 1875

46. HE 24th April,1869. (2¼ yards of broad cloth cost £1 8s. 8½d)

47. LM 26th October, 1833, advert for Parkton Grove. HC 18th January, 1851; the following year 'a large number of the workpeople' from the mill attended a new year treat at the pub HC 17th January, 1852; Agnes' sampler HC 7th June, 1851 (Thanks to David Pattern for this reference and the census returns. See also https://huddersfield.exposed/p/2319).

48. HC 2th February, 1856. See Mary Jagger, op.cit. pp. 149-154.

49. HC 24th October, 1868; HC 25th May, 1878 (Thanks to David Pattern for this reference).

50. HC 8th January, 1859

51. HC 27th July, 1861

52. HC 28th June et seq. 1862. For the background to the Antrobus riot see David Taylor, *Beerhouses, Brothels and Bobbies*. (*University of Huddersfield Press* 2016) especially pp.209-219. This was not the end of heavy handed policing: 'On Tuesday at the County Police court, Huddersfield, William Stephenson, iron turner, a native of Otley was charged with having wandered abroad for the purpose of begging alms at Magdale, South Crosland on Sunday afternoon. Sergeant Shuttleworth proved the case and the prisoner, who admitted that he had begged something to eat for his lad and himself, was sent to gaol for ten days – Superintendent Goodall said that the lad would be sent to the workhouse.' HEW 4th April, 1885.

53. HC 5th December,1863

54. HEW 22nd February, 1868

55. HE, HC, 28th October, 1865 (Abraham Mallinson lived until 1888 when he died age 63. His furniture and effects were auctioned off indicating he had outlived his wife, HEW 29th October, 1888.) HE 10th November, 1866, HC 7th September, 1867, HE 29th February, 1868, HE 15th May, 1871

56. HEW 28th December, 1878.

57. Censuses 1841-1851; *History of Meltham* Rev. Jos. Hughes pp.214-215; HC 2nd May, 1863, 7th May, 1881

58. Censuses 1861-1871; Honley Cemetery; York Probate registry; In the Huddersfield Naturalist Society (HNS) reports for the 1860's, Alfred's address appears as Greave House, Wilshaw. In 1864 he attended the ceremony of the cutting of the first sod of the Meltham railway. HC 9th April, 1864, HC 2nd November, 1867, Court Leet.

59. HEW 27th January, 1872; HC 25th January, 1873.

60. S. L. Mosley refers many times to Alfred Beaumont's collection, including in his *Birds of Huddersfield &c....* and often in an autobiographical context in one of his columns eg: 'Nature Study' December 1912; 'a History of the Huddersfield Museum' HEW 20th May, 1905; HEW 31st March, 1917; HEW 8th September,

1917; HEW 19th December, 1925. HEW 9th July, 1927.
61. HEW 31st August, 1878. He also had shooting rights over Lord Dartmouth's Hagg Wood at Honley. (HEW 20th May, 1876), Thomas Brooke's wood at Armitage Bridge and Black Moor, Linthwaite where game was preserved and watched by gamekeepers. HEW 9rd September, 3rd November,1877.
62. Op.cit. supra; Hemipode, Hobkirk, C.P. *History and Natural History of Huddersfield* 1868 Ed. ; Mosley, Birds, in 6d. Manual Series published at Beaumont Park, 1890s (Here he says it was reported in the Proceedings of the Zoological Society, 1860, p.210, which I have been unable to consult). He retracts this identification in HEW 14th August, 1915, 'Nature Around Huddersfield' (NAH) column; HEW 28 [th]April, 1917. Mary Jagger, *History of Honley* p.90; HEW 1st August, 1914.
63. Proceedings and Reports of HLSS and HNS for these periods, including 'Fifth Grand Exhibition of HNS', , HEW 11th October, 1873: HNS Exhibition.; HC 1st October, 1864: HEW 20th March and 11th December, 1875; HC 29th September, 1866.
64. HC 20th October, 1866. See also Alfred's obituary by GT Porritt's in *The Naturalist* 1st April, 1905 for du Chaillu and anecdotes about AB's personal qualities.
65. HEW 12th December, 1925; HEW 12th August, 1876; HEW 24th January, 1920.
66. HEW 25th June, 24 September1881; *Huddersfield Chronicle* 16th July, 1881. The Post Office was across the street from where it is now.
67. *Fine Arts and Industrial Exhibition* Catalogue pp 112-114. Mosley op.cit.1905, Stuart Davies *The Making of a Municipal Museum- Huddersfield and its Naturalists*, in Hilary Haigh, *A Most Handsome Town*. I am grateful for this article in guiding me from Alfred Beaumont to a full study of S.L. Mosley himself.
68. Michael Derby, *Biographical Dictionary of British Coleopterists'* (Internet); SLM HEW 19th December, 1925. After his departure from Huddersfield, Alfred became a notable entomologist publishing his first article *Captures of Coleoptera near Pitlochry, Perthshire* in the *Entomologists Monthly Magazine* in 1883.
69. The threatened closure of the Tolson Museum now puts the future of the bird collection in jeopardy.
70. HEW 12th May: Turner, Ben *Short History of the GUTW* (Heckmondwike 1920), HEW 9th May, 1891.
71. HEW 21st April, 1888.
72. HEW 22nd September, 1888; 2nd August, 6th September, 1890.
73. HE 15th January, 1870. HEW 20th May, 1893.
74. HE 25th January,1868 Cloth dressers treat. HEW 10th February, 1872, HEW 5th July, 1873.
75. HEW 6th February, 1886: The horse. 10th December, 1887, advert. 11th February, 1899: Ben's obituary.
76. HE 24th April, 1869 - (2¼ yards of broad cloth cost £1 8s. 8 ½ d). John Bentley Donkersley died in 1901 aged 58.
77. LM 27th November, 1847.
78. HC 3rd November, 1866.
79. HEW 29th July, 1876
80. HEW 27 February 1886, HEW 2nd January, HEW 16th January, HEW 30th October, 1892.
81. HEW 12th May; 1888
82. I am indebted to Sam's great-great-great grandson, Mr Geoff Horne of Sheffield, for these details.
83. HC 9th July, 1881.
84. HEW 24th February, 1883.
85. LM 5th March; 1814, HC 12th November, 1853; 20th March, 1852; HE 5th April, 1854; HC 15th August, 1868.
86. HE 24th December, 1870.
87. HEW 12th January, 1889; GT Porritt appears in the 1901 census at Crosland Hall.
88. HEW 1st April, 1870; HE 10th June, 1870; HEW 28th October, 1916 *Nature Around Huddersfield*, Jagger op.cit. p.90.
89. HE 16th May, 1868.
90. HC 15th August, 1868.
91. HEW 23rd July,1887.
92. HEW 9th October, 1897. The well is now in a sad state. The access track has been blocked off. Forgotten and ignored, this ancient site is steadily being reclaimed by nature. A new spring has erupted from the hillside a few yards away and the once gushing waters have been reduced to a trickle. Tree roots threaten to lever apart the stone work. It still retains a magical quality, but soon it will be too overgrown and dilapidated even for the fairies.
93. HEW 11th March, 1876 (LB); HC 23rd February, 1895 South Crosland UDC; HC 15th September, 1900 (Hillside yo let).
94. HEW 7th May; 21st May, 2nd July, 9th July, 1892. HEW 5th January, 6th July, 1901.
95. HEW 12th February, 1898; 7th May 1898. Nine case of scarlet fever at Magdale, only one at Netherton, patients moved to isolation hospital and houses fumigated. The outbreak continued into November. HEW 10th October, 7th Novovember, 1914.

96. Thanks to Geoffrey Fryer, freshwater biologist, for information about leeches.

97. HE 28th May, 1870.

98. HC 10th January, 24th January, 31st January, 7th February, 1863.

99. HC 21st March, 1863.

100. HC 17th September, 1881; HEW; 8th June, 29th July, 1893.

101. LM 25th April, 1822; HE 17th November, 1866; HE 8th February, 1868. In the parish register for 1559 the death of Wm Brigge of Helme is recorded when he was blown off his horse and drowned while crossing 'at a Hebble or narrow Brygge...' at 'Parke Mylne'. (Probably Park mill at Clayton West where there is still a pack horse bridge) There was another at Birkby for instance. HE 4th April, 1868.

102. HEW 11th November,1893; 7th July, 1894.

103. HEW 29th July, 2nd September, 4th November, 1899.

104. HEW 12th May, 1877; HEW 8th October, 1897; 11th May, 8th June, 1901; 11th January, 10th August,1902.

105. HEW 25th June, 1892.

106. *Northern Pioneer* 9th September, 1882.

107. HEW 10th January, 8th August, 12th September, 1914.

108. HEW 5th July, 1902; 24th December, 1904.

109. HEW 18th August, 1894.

110. HEW 6th February, HEW 3rd July, 1897.

111. HEW 26th January, 1895; HEW 22nd January, 1898; HEW 31st August, 1901 HExp, HEW 31st August, 1901.

112. YFT 16th November, 1901; HEW 27th November, 1902.

113. HEW 5th January, 1901.

114. YFT 10th and 14th November, 1902; 20th April, 1906: 26th June and 17th October, 1908. 29th July, 1909.

115. HEW 3rd July, 1909.

116. HEW 20th May, 1893.

117. HEW 22th April, 1901.

118. HEW 14th October, 1916. Oral information, Jeffrey Brooke.

119. HEW 2nd June, 1883, I am indebted to Magdale resident and musician David Bothwell for drawing my attention to the Elgar connection. The information is drawn from *August Jaeger: A Portrait of Nimrod – A life in Letters and other writings* Kevin Allen, (Ashgate 2000). There is also an article drawing on the recollections of Brian Tunstall in HED 18th August, 1966. A local tradition claims that Elgar himself visited Magdale, but I have found no confirmation of this. For more on Isabella Donkersley and John Tunstall see *Honley National School 1816-1952*, Peter Marshall, based on the research of Bob Etherington, published by Honley Civic Society 2016.

120. HEW 24th September to 22nd October, 1898.

121. HEW 17th April, 1917.

122. Membership book of Honley Socialist Club. Thanks to the late club secretary Mr Lewis Walker for access to this evidence.

123. HEW 4th November, 1916; 21st April, 1917.

124. HEW 28th October. 1916; 1st June, 1918.

125. HEW 5th May, 9th June, 1917.

126. HEW 5th May, 9th June, 1917. Two more members of the Honley Parish Church Bible class were killed the following year – Willis Bray (29) of Bradshaw Rd and Willie Shaw (19) of Swift Fold, HEW 13th April, 1918.

127. For more on Mark Brooke and other local COs see the Underground Histories website https://undergroundhistories.wordpress.com/the-white-feather-the-first-great-imperialist-war/

128. HEW 9th April, 8th October, 1927.

129. HEW 8th October, 1949; 17th January, 1948; 22nd August, 1936.

130. HEW 7th February, 1920; HED 8th December, 1948.

131. J W Tunstall died on 4th December, 1948 aged 83. HED 24th March, 1948.

132. For more on Honley Naturalists see Underground Histories website, https://undergroundhistories.wordpress.com/honley-naturalists-c-1860-1939/ Norman Brooke's name appears in the list of new members in the Naturalist the journal of the YNU in 1925, although his address is entered as 'Maydale'. Hamlet's obituary is in the Examiner's list for December 1939. Some of the other entries also describe the deceased by their accomplishments and interests rather than occupation, for example F L Farrand 'expert in grandfather clocks'. The recollections about Hamlet and Joe Allsop are also from Jeffrey Brooke. HED 11th December, 1939, Hamlet's inquest.

133. HEW 3rd June, 1950.